First published in the United States of America by
Rockport Publishers, a member of
Quayside Publishing Group
100 Cummings Center
Suite 406-L
Beverly, Massachusetts 01915-6101
Telephone: (978) 282-9590
Fax: (978) 283-2742
www.rockpub.com

Library of Congress Cataloging-in-Publication Data
1,000 music graphics : a compilation of packaging, posters, and other sound solutions / by Stoltze Design.
    p. cm.
  ISBN 1-59253-404-X
  1. Sound recordings--Album covers. I. Stoltze
Design. II. Title: One thousand music graphics.
  NC1882.A13 2008
  741.6'6--dc22
                                    2007041889

ISBN-13: 978-1-59253-404-3
ISBN-10: 1-59253-404-X

10 9 8 7 6 5 4 3 2 1

BOOK DESIGN
Stoltze Design, Boston
www.stoltze.com
ART DIRECTION
Clif Stoltze
DESIGN
Kyle Nelson
Lauren Vajda
DESIGN ASSISTANCE AND COORDINATION
Amanda Saulino
Melissa Crutcher
FONTS
DIN and Clarendon

Printed in China

BEVERLY MASSACHUSETTS

ROCKPORT PUBLISHERS

1000 Music Graphics

A compilation of packaging, posters, and other sound solutions

STOLTZENOISƎD

Contents

Many thanks to my staff, colleagues, and friends for their assistance and patience throughout this project, especially Kyle Nelson, Amanda Saulino, Lauren Vajda, Roy Burns, Mary Ross, Melissa Crutcher, Martin Sorger, Rudy Ruderman, and my family, Carol, Fiona, and Nick Stoltze. Special thanks to Zacron for the cover inspiration.

Introduction

For me, and countless other designers I've known, music and music graphics have been an unending source of inspiration. As a teenager, before I even knew what graphic design was, I thought there could be no greater artistic achievement than creating a Beatles or Rolling Stones album cover. It was my love of these legendary bands and their legendary album art that ultimately led me to become a graphic designer.

For nearly seventy years, music graphics have been instrumental in documenting and helping to define the evolution of both the musical landscape and popular culture. Even now, as the music industry struggles to cope with new formats and profit demands, design for music continues to be a hotbed for innovative and experimental graphics and typography. Much like its close relative, book jacket design, the appeal of music graphics for most designers lies in its ability to bridge the gap between art and commerce.

Beginning in the late 1930s, with the covers of Alex Steinweiss (arguably, the godfather of the record sleeve), music graphics were conceived primarily as a marketing tool aimed at helping the mostly 10", 78 rpm releases of a then-fledgling Columbia Records stand apart from the competition's standard, blank, brown paper sleeves (in an era when records were often purchased at the neighborhood hardware store).

In the late 1940s, the cover's canvas would both contract and expand with the advent of two new formats: the 45 rpm EP, and the 33 1/3 rpm LP. At 12" x 12", the LP cover was a virtual poster that still functioned primarily to promote the release while providing the listener with song and artist information. In the 1950s, savvier labels such as legendary jazz imprint Blue Note began using the LP sleeve as a way to cultivate a recognizable brand that listeners could trust, thus encouraging them to take a chance on anything bearing the Blue Note mark (and Reid Miles' distinctive designs). For lovers of pop and the newly minted genre of rock and roll, the quick and portable 7" x 7" 45—now primarily used to showcase single songs—would become the format of choice, and remain so well into the 1960s.

As both rock and roll and its audience matured, so did its artists. The dominance of the 45 was challenged as more innovative groups, like The Beatles, began using the long-playing album for the creation of fully formed artistic statements. As a result, the decade saw an amazing explosion in album art. During the psychedelic era of the late 1960s, sleeve designers such as Mati Klarwein and Martin Sharp, along with poster artists including Victor Moscoso, Stanley Mouse, and Alton Kelley created visual feasts that you could stare at for hours.

Many consider the 1970s as the heyday of album cover art. The budgets were big and the work attracted and supported some of the most celebrated artists of the time. Alongside work by design studios like London-based Hipgnosis, which specialized in high-concept album art for groups like Pink Floyd and Led Zeppelin, artists such as Andy Warhol, Richard Avedon, and even Norman Rockwell were recruited (and paid handsomely) to create record covers.

In the late 1970s, as the record industry had grown big, bloated, and flush with excess, punk music broke out, embodying a subversive "do-it-yourself" ethos. England's Sex Pistols quickly came to epitomize the movement and Jamie Reid's cover for the album, *Never Mind the Bollocks, Here's the Sex Pistols* became an icon of the time. While this approach—along with many other of punk's most notorious

fashion statements—would become cliché almost overnight, Reid had created a visually memorable style that could be done quickly and easily, with limited technical know-how—much like punk music itself.

In the wake of punk, this DIY attitude led to the proliferation of thousands of bands and hundreds of independent record labels. During the tail end of the decade and into the early 1980s, some of these labels, namely the United Kingdom's Factory and 4AD labels, would become as renowned and influential for their visual output as they were for the music of their artists. For Factory, designer Peter Saville's restrained, impeccably crafted graphics for artists like Joy Division, New Order, and Section 25 stood in stark contrast to the punk and trendy new wave graphics of the day. While Factory's early sleeves were exercises in calculated coolness, Vaughan Oliver's sleeves for 4AD bands such as Cocteau Twins, Dead Can Dance, and This Mortal Coil were far more lush and enigmatic. Like the music, Oliver's sleeves would also gain a devoted fan base, which enticed fans into buying 4AD releases sound unheard.

When the compact disc format first appeared in 1982, album cover real estate was suddenly reduced to a third of the size of an LP. Designers grappled with these new constraints by all but ignoring them, continuing to design for the LP and then reducing to fit. But as CDs gradually became the medium of choice for consumers, some designers like Stefan Sagmeister recognized its possibilities. Well-known for his unconventional approach to design, typography, and imagery, Sagmeister once stated that what the CD cover lacked in size, it more than made up for in the potential for depth made possible through additional panels and pages. Unlike the LP, the compact size enabled designers to outwardly ignore its industry-standard jewel case package Sagmeister's 2003 Talking Heads compilation, *Once in a Lifetime* (see page 105), confronts industry notions on the commercial viability of non-standard forms of packaging.

Today, many burgeoning music fans don't own CDs, but instead choose to buy (borrow and steal) their music online—and wear that badge proudly. Since the convenience of the digital download has yet to pair with a captivating, downloadable equivalent of the CD package, bands and labels have in turn amped up their online presence, resulting in some truly noteworthy design. Ed Mullen, with his collaged approach for bands like Blanche (see page 275), manages to cleverly combine the simulated tactile appeal of print with the added attraction of interactivity, to truly engaging effect.

In recent years, at least in part as a response to the oft-heralded demise of album art, the poster has undergone a virtual renaissance—specifically, independent silk-screen artists creating gig posters for venues of all sizes. Continuing in the tradition of the rock posters of the 1960s, this current movement has become a cottage industry, with designers creating their own product and selling it online and through various independent record stores. Included here are striking examples—from studios such as Aesthetic Apparatus, The Small Stakes, and Patent Pending, featuring the work of Sub Pop art director Jeff Kleinsmith—that have helped create a broader audience for this art form.

While much of the music packaging from major labels these days veers toward the proven and formulaic, intended to maximize visual presence on sales racks and retain that presence as postage stamp-sized images on MP3 players and websites, there are exceptions. One artist whose craft and attention to detail often extends to the presentation of his music is Beck, whose recent CD, *The Information*, is an example of the recent interest by labels and artists in adding value to the non-downloadable music purchasing experience. Designed by London's Big Active, *The Information* seeks to engage the listener in the design process itself (see page 17). With *The Information*, the fan is provided with a toolkit of stickers and a gridded, semi-blank canvas to create their own cover. Interestingly, upon release it was denied access to the United Kingdom's CD sales charts when its inclusion of this set of stickers, as well as a DVD, was deemed to have given it an

unfair advantage over other albums released that week (absurdly assuming that the sales potential of all music is on a level playing field without its accompanying artwork).

Perhaps this, then, is the designer's role and responsibility—to create an "unfair advantage" by employing innovative ideas that add value to the product, helping it rise above a sea of conventionality. This collection of over 1,000 examples of music packaging, posters, and other ephemera serves as both an overview and a celebration of work that has, over the past decade, done just that. Collected through a public call for entries and by invitation, we quickly amassed much more good work than we could feature in this not-so-slim volume. Many, many thanks to all who submitted their work, whether included here or not. It is my hope that this book serves as a valuable resource and inspiration for design and music aficionados everywhere.

Clif Stoltze

10

Chapter 1

Packaging

CD, DVD, vinyl, and other musical packaging experiences

0001-0524

P1

0002 ▶ **Sub Pop Records,** USA

0003 ▶ **Sub Pop Records,** USA

0004 ▶ **Sub Pop Records,** USA

0005 ▶ **Sub Pop Records,** USA

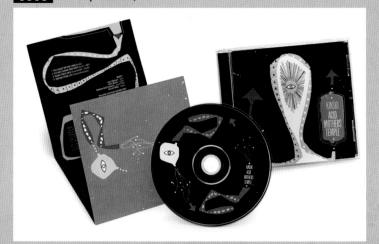

0006 ▶ **Sub Pop Records,** USA

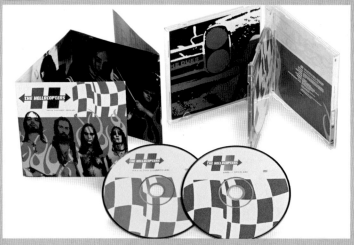

0007 Art Chantry Design, USA

0008 Art Chantry Design, USA

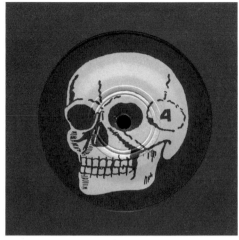

0009 Art Chantry Design, USA

0010 Art Chantry Design, USA

0011 Art Chantry Design, USA

0012 Art Chantry Design, USA

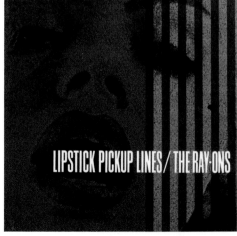

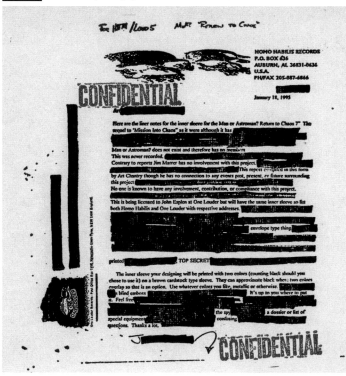

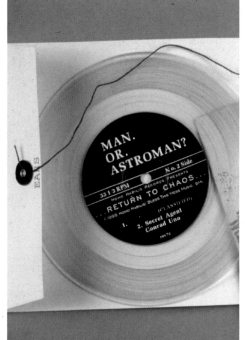

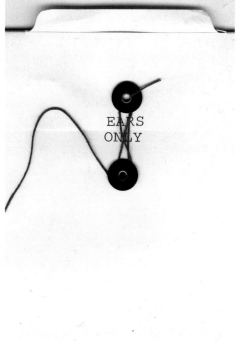

0018 ▶ Big Active, UK

KEANE
UNDER
THE
IRON
SEA

0019 ▶ Big Active, UK

KEANE
IS IT ANY
WONDER?

0020 ▶ Big Active, UK

KEANE
TRY AGAIN

0021 ▶ Big Active, UK

KEANE
CRYSTAL
BALL

KEANE
A BAD
DREAM

0023 ▶ Big Active, UK

0024 ▶ Big Active, UK

0025 ▶ Big Active, UK

0026 ▶ Big Active, UK

0028 ▶ **Yokoland,** Norway

0029 ▶ **Yokoland,** Norway

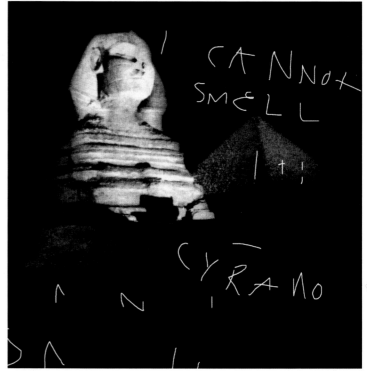

0030 ▶ **Yokoland,** Norway

0031 ▶ **Yokoland,** Norway

0034 Human Empire, Germany

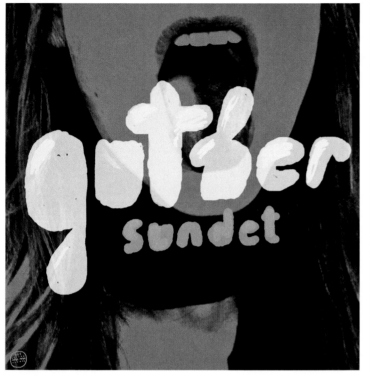

0035 Human Empire, Germany

0036 Human Empire, Germany

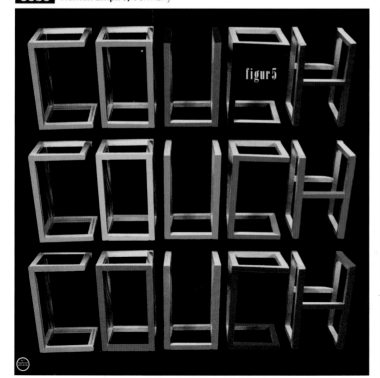

0037 Human Empire, Germany

0038 ▸ **FPM Factor Product GMBH,** Germany

0039 ▸ **FPM Factor Product GMBH,** Germany

0040 ▸ **FPM Factor Product GMBH,** Germany

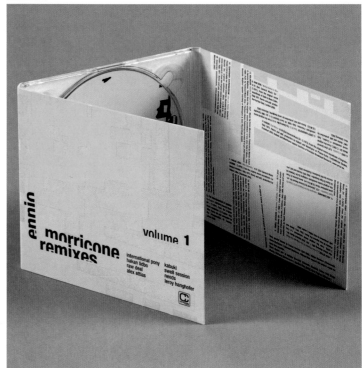

0041 ▶ **FPM Factor Product GMBH,** Germany

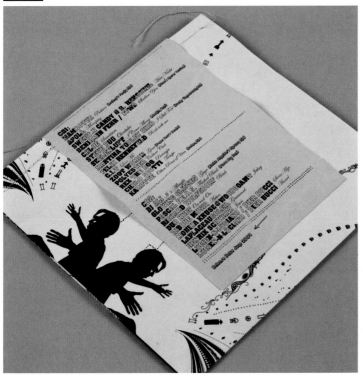

0042 ▶ **FPM Factor Product GMBH,** Germany

0043 ▶ **FPM Factor Product GMBH,** Germany

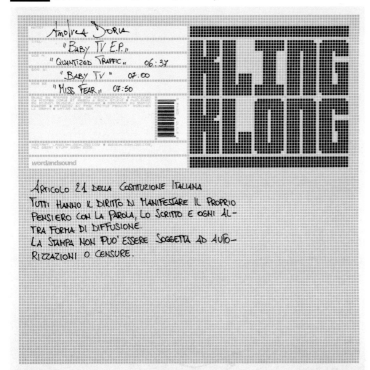

0044 ▶ **FPM Factor Product GMBH,** Germany

0045 ▶ Tom Hingston Studio, UK

0046 ▶ Tom Hingston Studio, UK

0047 ▶ Tom Hingston Studio, UK

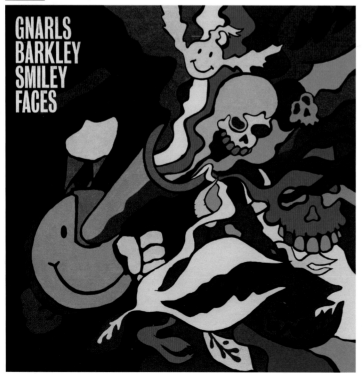

0048 ▶ Tom Hingston Studio, UK

0050 ▶ **LeDouxville,** USA

0051 ▶ **LeDouxville,** USA

0052 ▶ **LeDouxville,** USA

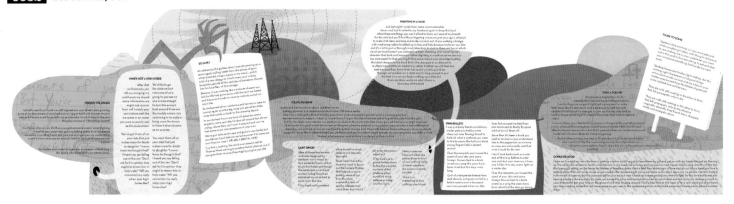

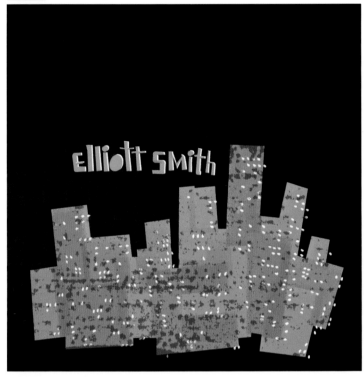

0057 ▶ **Stefan Kassel Design,** Germany

LEE HAZLEWOOD

For Every Solution There's A Problem

0058 Stefan Kassel Design, Germany

Ave Marina™

0059 Stefan Kassel Design, Germany

BOSSA NOVA

★ ★ ★ ★ ★ ★ ★

THE SOUND OF IPANEMA

0060 Stefan Kassel Design, Germany

THE GET EASY! SUNSHINE POP COLLECTION

0061 Stefan Kassel Design, Germany

AMIGA A GO-GO

VOL. 1: DEUTSCH-DEMOKRATISCHE RARE GROOVES

THEO SCHUMANN COMBO · USCHI BRÜHNING · MANFRED KRUG · ORCHESTER WALTER KUBICZECK · GÜNTHER FISCHER · CHRIS DOERK & UVE SCHIKORA COMBO · KLAUS LENZ · REINHARD LAKOMY · GERD MICHAELIS CHOR · MODERN SOUL BAND · EVGENI KANTSCHEV · VERONIKA FISCHER & BAND · PANTA RHEI · ORCHESTER GÜNTER GOLLASCH

0062 Stefan Kassel Design, Germany

AMIGA A GO-GO

VOL. 2: DEUTSCH-DEMOKRATISCHER BEAT

THEO SCHUMANN COMBO · DRESDEN SEXTETT · MANFRED KRUG · SKALDOWIE · HORST KRÜGER SEXTETT · TEAM 4 · DIE SPUTNIKS · MANFRED LUDWIG SEPTETT · THOMAS NATSCHINSKI & GRUPPE · DIE ALEXANDERS · GERD MICHAELIS CHOR · THOMAS LÜCK · ILLES · ROTE GITARREN · DIE BEROLINAS · BALTIC QUINTETT

0063 Stefan Kassel Design, Germany

AMIGA A GO-GO

VOL. 3: DEUTSCH-DEMOKRATISCHE SOUNDTRACKS

EAST GERMAN FILM AND TV THEMES BY WALTER KUBICZECK · INCL. HEISSE SPUR · TENTAKEL · MASKENTANZ · KING-KONG · FEUERDRACHEN · REGENBOGEN · NEBEL · TIGERAUGE · FAHNDUNG · ROTIGOR · EL PARAISO · AUDIOVISION · EXOTICA · ABISSINIA · ELDORADO · VISION · SAVANNE · KALAHARI · TSCHÜSS PT. I & II

0064 ▶ **Stefan Kassel Design,** Germany

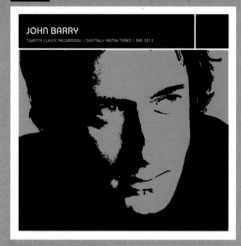

JOHN BARRY
TWENTY CLASSIC RECORDINGS / DIGITALLY REMASTERED / 585 317-2

0065 ▶ **Stefan Kassel Design,** Germany

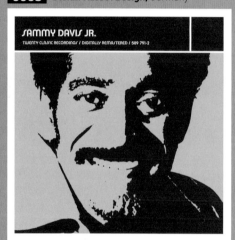

BURT BACHARACH
TWENTY CLASSIC RECORDINGS / DIGITALLY REMASTERED / 589 021-2

0066 ▶ **Stefan Kassel Design,** Germany

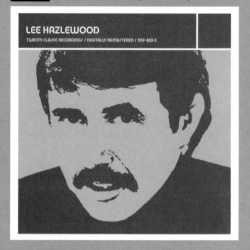

LEE HAZLEWOOD
TWENTY CLASSIC RECORDINGS / DIGITALLY REMASTERED / 559 882-2

0067 ▶ **Stefan Kassel Design,** Germany

ROBERTO DELGADO
TWENTY CLASSIC RECORDINGS / DIGITALLY REMASTERED / 549 677-2

0068 ▶ **Stefan Kassel Design,** Germany

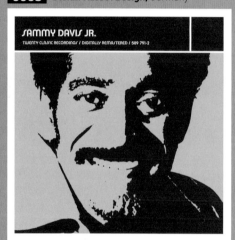

SAMMY DAVIS JR.
TWENTY CLASSIC RECORDINGS / DIGITALLY REMASTERED / 589 791-2

0069 ▶ **Stefan Kassel Design,** Germany

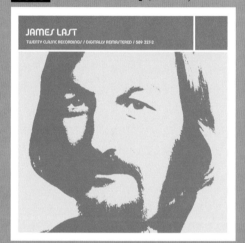

JAMES LAST
TWENTY CLASSIC RECORDINGS / DIGITALLY REMASTERED / 589 327-2

0070 ▶ **Stefan Kassel Design,** Germany

DUSTY SPRINGFIELD
TWENTY CLASSIC RECORDINGS / DIGITALLY REMASTERED / 586 469-2

0071 ▶ **Stefan Kassel Design,** Germany

GUNTER KALLMANN CHOIR
TWENTY CLASSIC RECORDINGS / DIGITALLY REMASTERED / 589 792-2

0072 ▶ **Stefan Kassel Design,** Germany

FRANCE GALL
TWENTY CLASSIC RECORDINGS / DIGITALLY REMASTERED / 589 727-2

0073 ▶ Stefan Kassel Design, Germany

the magic circles
meet me in milan

0074 ▶ Stefan Kassel Design, Germany

0075 ▶ Stefan Kassel Design, Germany

meet me in milan
you are the one

0076 ▶ Stefan Kassel Design, Germany

0077 ▶ Stefan Kassel Design, Germany

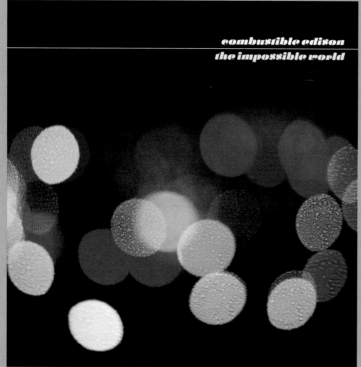

combustible edison
the impossible world

0078 ▶ Funnel: Eric Kass: Utilitarian + Commercial + Fine Art, USA

CCB-405 LOVE BEING HERE WITH YOU — COOL CITY BAND

HI-FI   **STEREOPHONIC**   **CCB-405**

Cool City Band **Featuring Shannon Forsell & Jimmy Guilford**
LOVE BEING HERE
Conducted by Roy Geesa   *WITH YOU*

0079 ▶ Tom Hingston Studio, UK

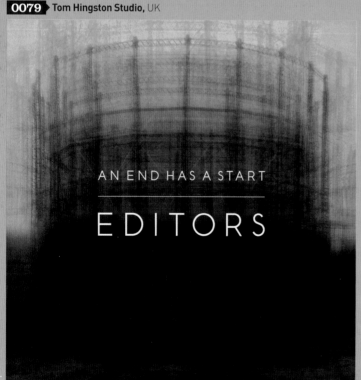

AN END HAS A START

EDITORS

0080 ▶ Tom Hingston Studio, UK

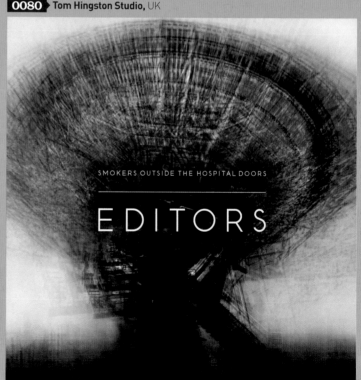

SMOKERS OUTSIDE THE HOSPITAL DOORS

EDITORS

0081 ▶ **Stoltze Design,** USA

OHM :the early gurus of electronic music :1948–1980

MARYANNE AMACHER
ROBERT ASHLEY
MILTON BABBITT
LOUIS AND BEBE BARRON
FRANCOIS BAYLE
DAVID BEHRMAN
JOHN CAGE
JOHN CHOWNING
ALVIN CURRAN
HOLGER CZUKAY
TOD DOCKSTADER
CHARLES DODGE
HERBERT EIMERT
ROBERT BEYER
BRIAN ENO
LUC FERARRI
JON HASSELL
PAUL LANSKY
HUGH LE CAINE
ALVIN LUCIER
OTTO LUENING
RICHARD MAXFIELD
OLIVIER MESSIAEN
MEV
PAULINE OLIVEROS
BERNARD PARMEGIANI
STEVE REICH
TERRY RILEY
JEAN-CLAUDE RISSET
CLARA ROCKMORE
OSKAR SALA
PIERRE SCHAEFFER
KLAUS SCHULZE
RAYMOND SCOTT
LAURIE SPIEGEL
KARLHEINZ STOCKHAUSEN
MORTON SUBOTNICK
DAVID TUDOR
VLADIMIR USSACHEVSKY
EDGARD VARESE
IANNIS XENAKIS
LA MONTE YOUNG
JOJI YUASA

0082 ▶ **Stoltze Design,** USA

OHM+ :the early gurus of electronic music :1948–1980

SPECIAL EDITION 3CD + DVD

MARYANNE AMACHER
ROBERT ASHLEY
MILTON BABBITT
LOUIS AND BEBE BARRON
FRANCOIS BAYLE
DAVID BEHRMAN
JOHN CAGE
JOHN CHOWNING
ALVIN CURRAN
HOLGER CZUKAY
TOD DOCKSTADER
CHARLES DODGE
HERBERT EIMERT
ROBERT BEYER
BRIAN ENO
LUC FERARRI
JON HASSELL
PAUL LANSKY
HUGH LE CAINE
ALVIN LUCIER
OTTO LUENING
RICHARD MAXFIELD
OLIVIER MESSIAEN
MEV
PAULINE OLIVEROS
BERNARD PARMEGIANI
STEVE REICH
TERRY RILEY
JEAN-CLAUDE RISSET
CLARA ROCKMORE
OSKAR SALA
PIERRE SCHAEFFER
KLAUS SCHULZE
RAYMOND SCOTT
LAURIE SPIEGEL
KARLHEINZ STOCKHAUSEN
MORTON SUBOTNICK
DAVID TUDOR
VLADIMIR USSACHEVSKY
EDGARD VARESE
IANNIS XENAKIS
LA MONTE YOUNG
JOJI YUASA

0083 ▶ **Stoltze Design,** USA

0084 Stoltze Design, USA

0085 Stoltze Design, USA

0086 Stoltze Design, USA

0087 ▶ **Rehab Design,** USA

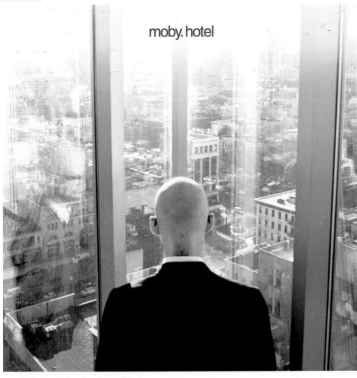

moby. hotel

0088 ▶ **Rehab Design,** USA

and my hope in this record is not to celebrate or represent the vacuum-like neutrality of an empty hotel room, but rather to represent the part of the human condition that compels us to read big and expansive and messy biological lives. i'm fascinated by the airless and lifeless neutrality of so many man-made spaces empty airports, empty lobbies, empty office

buildings, etc). but i don't feel like making music that is airless and lifeless because i also really like people and the messy miasma of the human condition and i want to make messy, human records that are open and emotional, because, whether i like it or not,

0089 ▶ **Rehab Design,** USA

MOBY·HOTEL
AMBIENT

0090 ▶ **Rehab Design,** USA

MOBY·HOTEL

0091 ▶ **Rehab Design,** USA

i'm messy and human, too
(even though like all good
sci-fi geeks i do occasionally
wish that i was a robot).
have i said too much?
should i err on the side
of cryptic and esoteric
explanations?

well, this explanation is
neither cryptic nor esoteric,
so there you go.
and that's why the record
is called 'hotel'.
thanks, and i hope that you
like what you hear.
moby

0092 ▶ **Angela Lorenz,** Germany

folie eyepennies

0093 ▶ **Angela Lorenz,** Germany

0094 ▶ **Angela Lorenz,** Germany

0095 ▶ **Angela Lorenz,** Germany

0096 ▶ **Angela Lorenz,** Germany

0097 ▶ **Angela Lorenz,** Germany

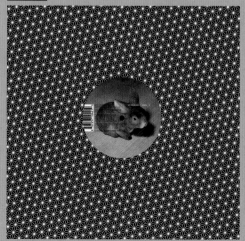

0098 ▸ **Angela Lorenz,** Germany

FULL SWING [EDITS]

0099 ▸ **Angela Lorenz,** Germany

FULL SWING [EDITS]

0100 ▸ **Angela Lorenz,** Germany

FULL SWING [EDITS]

0101 ▸ **Angela Lorenz,** Germany

FULL SWING [EDITS]

0102 ▸ **Angela Lorenz,** Germany

FULL SWING [EDITS]

0103 ▸ **Angela Lorenz,** Germany

FULL SWING [EDITS]

0104 ▸ **Angela Lorenz,** Germany

FULL SWING [EDITS]

0105 ▸ **Angela Lorenz,** Germany

FULL SWING [EDITS]

0106 ▸ **Angela Lorenz,** Germany

FULL SWING [EDITS]

0107 ▸ **Yacht Associates,** UK

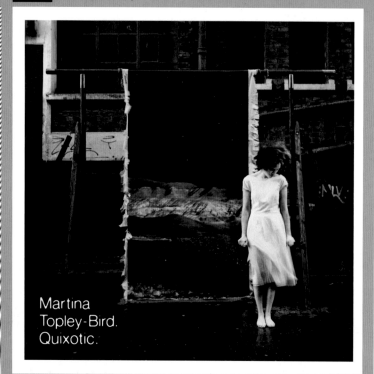

Martina
Topley-Bird.
Quixotic.

0108 ▸ **Yacht Associates,** UK

Martina.
Topley-Bird.
I Still Feel.

0109 ▸ **Yacht Associates,** UK

Martina Topley Bird. Need One.

0110 ▸ **Yacht Associates,** UK

Martina
Topley-Bird.
Soul Food.

0111 ▶ Yacht Associates, UK

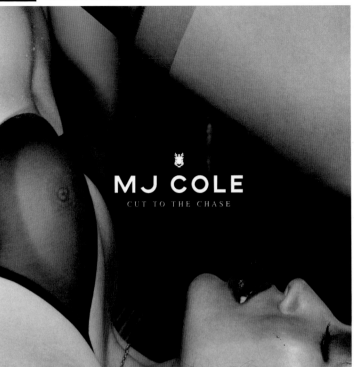

0112 ▶ Yacht Associates, UK

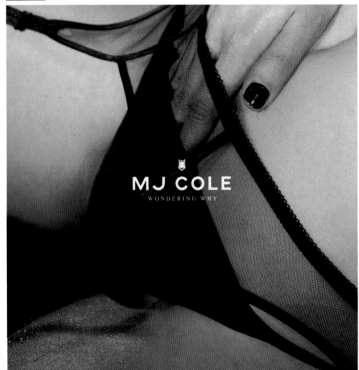

0113 ▶ Yacht Associates, UK

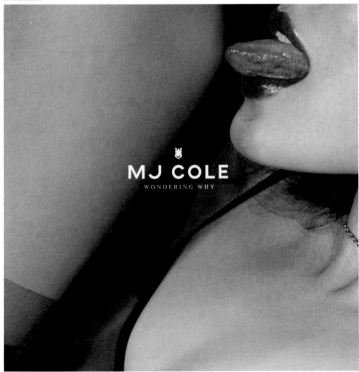

0114 ▶ Yacht Associates, UK

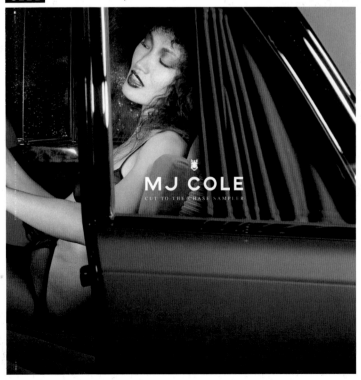

0115 ▶ Tom Hingston Studio, UK

0116 ▶ Tom Hingston Studio, UK

0117 ▶ Tom Hingston Studio, UK

0118 ▶ Tom Hingston Studio, UK

0119 Tom Hingston Studio, UK

Nick Cave
& The Bad Seeds
Abattoir Blues

0120 ▶ **desres design group,** Germany

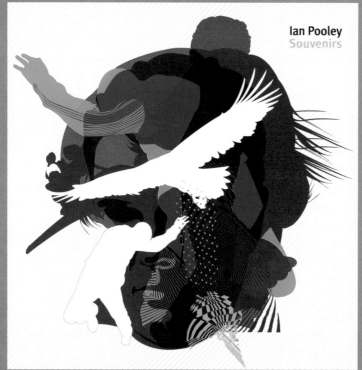

Ian Pooley
Souvenirs

0121 ▶ **desres design group,** Germany

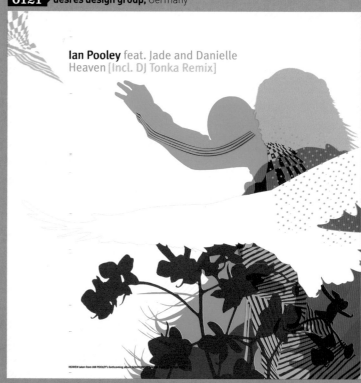

Ian Pooley feat. Jade and Danielle
Heaven [Incl. DJ Tonka Remix]

0122 ▶ **desres design group,** Germany

RETURNED no 02 /
CELTIC CROSS /
IAN POOLEY / TONKA /
ZOO BRAZIL /

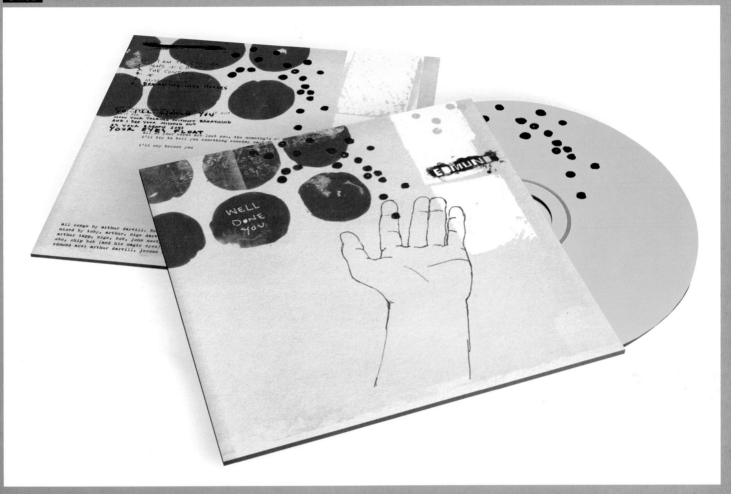

0126 ▶ Big Active, UK

ATHLETE
TOURIST

0127 ▶ Big Active, UK

PROTOCOL
RULES OF
engagement

0128 ▶ Scott King, UK

PET
SHOP
BOYS
London

0129 ▶ Scott King, UK

PET
SHOP
BOYS

Home and dry

0130 Form, UK

イ・ビ・ティ・ジー **EVERYTHING BUT THE GIRL**
WRONG

0131 Form, UK

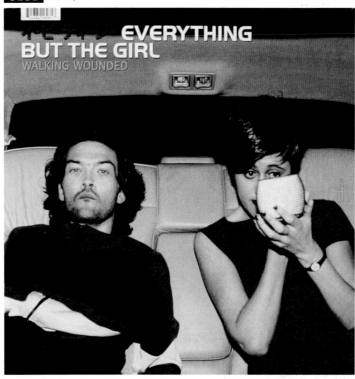

EVERYTHING BUT THE GIRL
WALKING WOUNDED

0132 Form, UK

イ・ビ・ティ・ジー **EVERYTHING BUT THE GIRL**
WALKING WOUNDED

0133 Form, UK

0134 Yacht Associates, UK

0135 Yacht Associates, UK

0136 Yacht Associates, UK

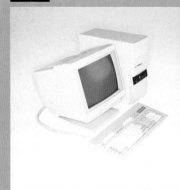

0137 Yacht Associates, UK

0138 Yacht Associates, UK

0139 Yacht Associates, UK

0140 ▸ Form, UK

0141 ▸ Form, UK

0142 ▸ Form, UK

0143 ▸ Form, UK

0144 ▸ Aesthetic Apparatus, USA

0145 ▸ Richard May, UK

0146 ▸ Four5One°Creative, Ireland

0147 ▸ Aesthetic Apparatus, USA

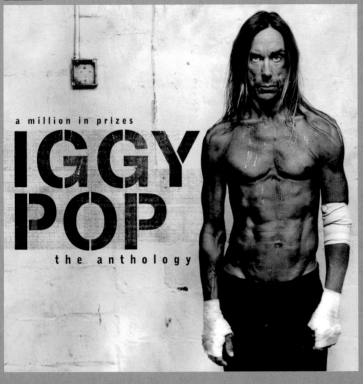

a million in prizes
IGGY POP
the anthology

This recording and artwork are protected by copyright law. Using Internet services to distribute copyrighted music, giving away illegal copies of discs or lending discs to others for them to copy is illegal and does not support those involved in making this piece of music – especially the artist. By carrying out any of these actions it has the same effect as stealing music. Applicable laws provide severe civil and criminal penalties for the unauthorized reproduction, distribution and digital transmission of copyrighted sound recordings. Many examples of where to buy legal downloads can be found at www.musicfromemi.com

0150 ▶ Undaunted, USA

0151 ▶ Undaunted, USA

STÒ CAZZO!

SWEEP THE LEG JOHNNY

SWEEPTHS

STOCAZZ

SOUTHERN RECORDS P.O. BOX 577375 CHICAGO IL 60657 USA
P.O. BOX 59 LONDON N22 1AR ENGLAND   SOUTHERN 18568-1   MADE IN ENGLAND

0152 ▶ **Four50ne°Creative,** Ireland

U2 ALL THAT YOU CAN'T LEAVE BEHIND

0153 ▶ **Four50ne°Creative,** Ireland

0154 ▶ **Four50ne°Creative,** Ireland

0155 ▶ **Four50ne°Creative,** Ireland

0156 ▶ **Four5One°Creative,** Ireland

0157 ▶ **Four5One°Creative,** Ireland

0158 ▶ **Four5One°Creative,** Ireland

0159 ▶ **Four5One°Creative,** Ireland

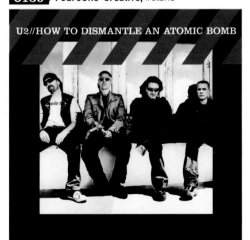

0160 ▶ **Four5One°Creative,** Ireland

0161 ▶ Rinzen, Australia

0162 ▶ Rinzen, Australia

0163 ▶ Rinzen, Australia

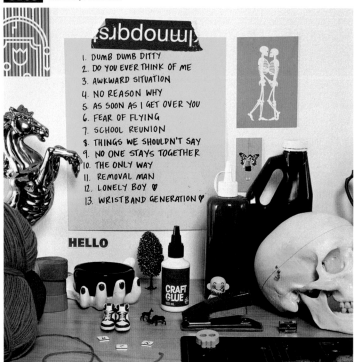

0164 ▶ Rinzen, Australia

0165 ▶ Rune Mortensen Design Studio, Norway

New studio album
**THE THING
ACTION JAZZ**

Mats Gustafsson
Ingebrigt Håker Flaten
Paal Nilssen-Love

«The sheer power they gene-
rate from wood, metal, breath
and muscle is stunning»
BBC

«The Thing convert nouveau
punk and vintage garage
rock into a roaring scream-
up, but the sheer energy
and love of the music keep
gimmickry at bay»
UNCUT

SMJZ
www.smalltownsuperjazzz.com
STSJ123CD

0166 ▶ Rune Mortensen Design Studio, Norway

**TWO
BANDS
AND A
LEGEND**

**FEATURING
CATO SALSA EXPERIENCE
AND THE THING
WITH JOE McPHEE**
LINERNOTES BY
THURSTON MOORE

STSJ104CD

0167 ▶ Rune Mortensen Design Studio, Norway

**KEN VANDERMARK
PAAL NILSSEN-LOVE
SEVEN**

1. First Hit, Second Fall (26:36)
2. Open Too Close (14:03)
3. Universal Funeral (3:19)

Ken Vandermark, tenor and baritone saxophone, Bb clarinet
Paal Nilssen-Love, drums and percussion

All compositions by Vandermark (ASCAP) and Nilssen-Love
(TONO/NCB). Recorded live at Blå on April the 1st,
mixed on December the 13th 2005 by Thomas Hukkelberg
at desibel.no. Live sound by Stig Gunnar Ringen. Produced
by Ken Vandermark and Paal Nilssen-Love. Co-produced by
Joakim Haugland. Photos and design by Rune Mortensen.
This recording is dedicated to Bjørnar Andresen.

www.smalltownsuperjazz.com

SMJZ
6 00116 84192   N©B   STSJ119CD
©© SMALLTOWNSUPERJAZZZ 2006

All rights of the
producer and of the owner
of the work reproduced
reserved. Unauthorised
copying, hiring, lending,
public performance
and broadcasting of this
record prohibited.

0168 ▶ Big Active, UK

0169 ▶ **Four5One°Creative,** Ireland

0170 ▶ **Four5One°Creative,** Ireland

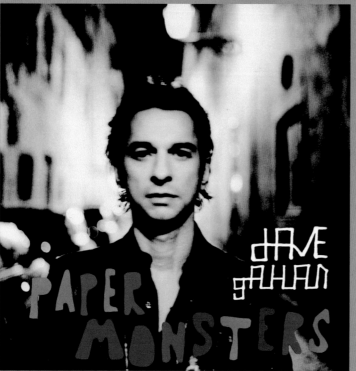

0171 ▶ **Four5One°Creative,** Ireland

0172 ▶ **Four5One°Creative**, Ireland

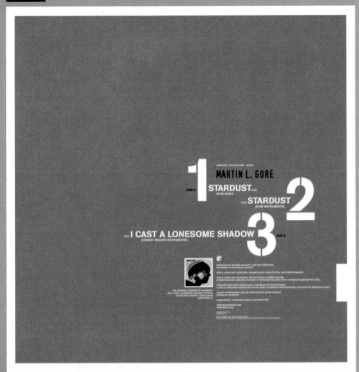

0173 ▶ **Four5One°Creative**, Ireland

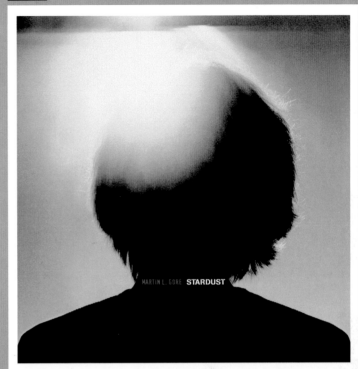

0174 ▶ **Four5One°Creative**, Ireland

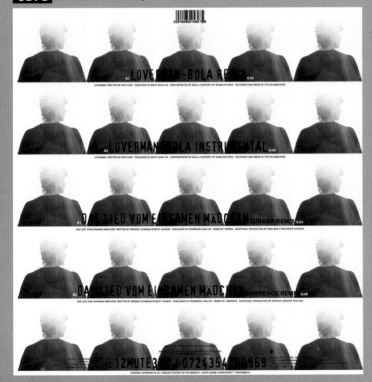

0175 ▶ **Four5One°Creative**, Ireland

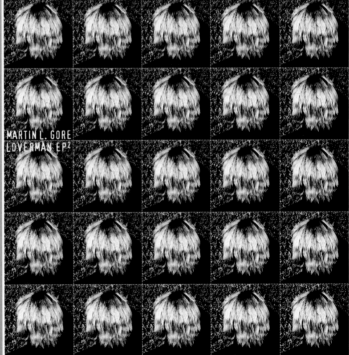

0176 ▶ **Form**, UK

0177 ▶ **Form**, UK

187 LOCKDOWN.

0178 ▶ **Form**, UK

One way

No parking in front of these gates

187 LOCKDOWN.
GUNMAN

0179 ▶ **Form**, UK

0180 ▶ **Form**, UK

0181 ▶ **Form**, UK

187 LOCKDOWN.
THE DON

0182 ▶ **Ghost Ranch Studio,** Japan

0183 ▶ **Ghost Ranch Studio,** Japan

0184 ▶ **Ghost Ranch Studio,** Japan

0185 ▶ **Ghost Ranch Studio,** Japan

0186 ▶ Big Active, UK

simian
the wisp
(ep)

0187 ▶ Big Active, UK

simian
one dimension
(ep)

0188 ▶ Big Active, UK

simian
mr. crow
(ep)

0189 ▶ Big Active, UK

simian
chemistry is what we are
(lp)

0190 ▶ Segura, Inc., USA

0191 ▶ FPM Factor Product GMBH, Germany

0192 ▶ JSDS, USA

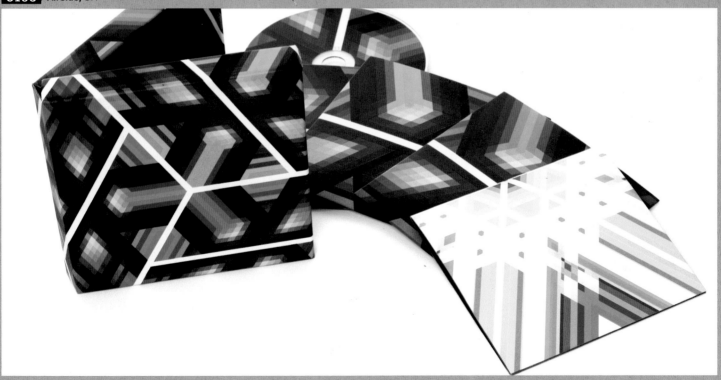

0197 ▶ **Karim Rashid, Inc.,** USA

0198 ▶ **Kymtra Design,** USA

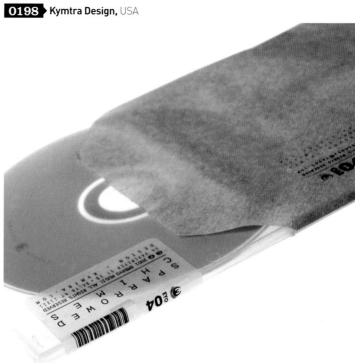

0199 ▶ **Kim Hiorthøy,** Norway

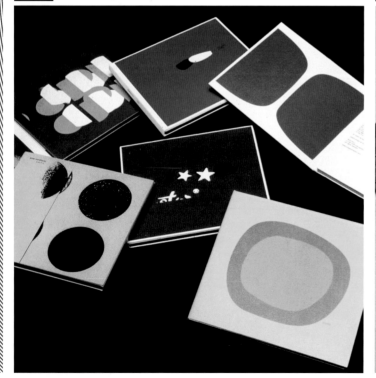

0200 ▶ **Power of Beauty Co., Ltd.,** Japan

0201 ▶ LeDouxville, USA

0202 ▶ LeBoYe, Indonesia

0203 ▶ Power of Beauty Co., Ltd., Japan

0204 ▶ Chen Design Associates, USA

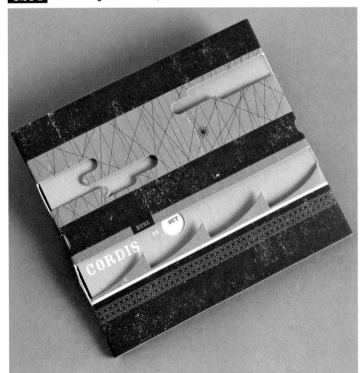

1. PERFORMANCE 2 TIME: 68:54. CD 2. PERFORMANCE 4 TIME: 66:57. CD 3. PERFORMANCE 5 TIME: 62:26 RECORDED LIVE IN THREE TAKES WITH:

TOTAL PLAYING TIME OF ALL THREE DISCS: 3:18:17 Ⓟ&© 2001 COMPOSERS RECORDINGS, INC. 73 SPRING STREET, SUITE 506, NEW YORK, N.Y. 10012 PHONE (212) 941-9673 WWW.COMPOSERSRECORDINGS.COM (CRI LOGO) (BLUESHIFT LOGO) CD 2001 DDD (COMPACT DISC LOGO) THE BARCODE IS LOCATED ON THE SPINE

0209 ▸ karlssonwilker inc., USA

0210 ▸ karlssonwilker inc., USA

0211 ▸ karlssonwilker inc., USA

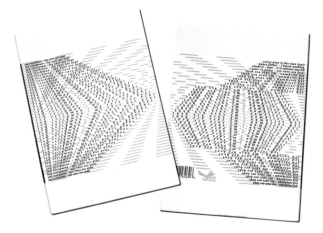

0212 ▸ karlssonwilker inc., USA

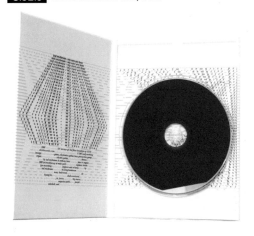

0213 ▸ karlssonwilker inc., USA

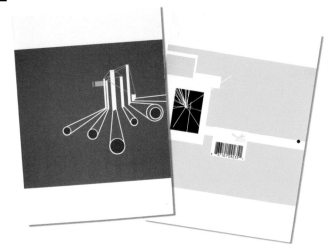

0214 ▸ karlssonwilker inc., USA

0216 Jutojo, Germany

0217 Jutojo, Germany

0218 Jutojo, Germany

0219 Jutojo, Germany

0220 ▶ Red Design, UK

0221 ▶ Red Design, UK

0222 ▶ Red Design, UK

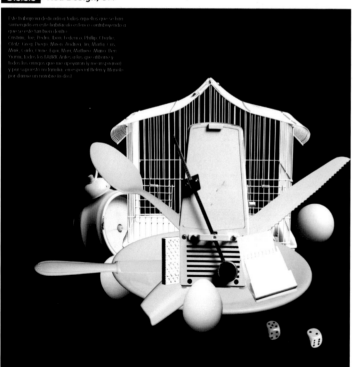

0223 ▶ Red Design, UK

0227 ▶ Power of Beauty Co., Ltd., Japan

0228 ▶ Power of Beauty Co., Ltd., Japan

0229 Me Company LTD, UK

0230 Me Company LTD, UK

0231 Me Company LTD, UK

0232 Me Company LTD, UK

0233 Me Company LTD, UK

0234 Me Company LTD, UK

0235 Me Company LTD, UK

0236 Me Company LTD, UK

0237 Me Company LTD, UK

0238 ▶ Me Company LTD, UK

0239 ▶ Me Company LTD, UK

0240 ▶ Me Company LTD, UK

0241 ▶ Me Company LTD, UK

0242 ▶ Me Company LTD, UK

0243 ▶ Me Company LTD, UK

0244 ▶ Me Company LTD, UK

0245 ▶ Me Company LTD, UK

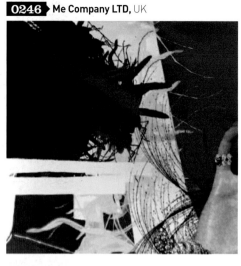

0246 ▶ Me Company LTD, UK

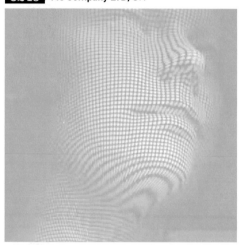

0247 ▶ Me Company LTD, UK

0248 ▶ Me Company LTD, UK

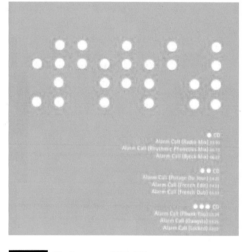

0249 ▶ Me Company LTD, UK

0250 ▶ Me Company LTD, UK

0251 ▶ Me Company LTD, UK

0252 ▶ Me Company LTD, UK

01 SWING UR SOUL
02 VOICELESS
03 BASS CAMP
04 DELHI NEWS
05 EXOTICA
06 NOËL
07 ROUNDHOUSE
08 DOWN SOUTH
09 THE SAYING
10 NAOMI

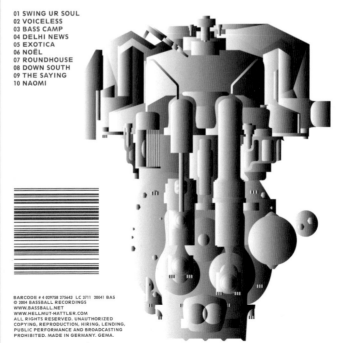

BARCODE # 4 029758 275643 LC 3711 20041 BAS
© 2004 BASSBALL RECORDINGS
WWW.BASSBALL.NET
WWW.HELLMUT-HATTLER.COM
ALL RIGHTS RESERVED. UNAUTHORIZED
COPYING, REPRODUCTION, HIRING, LENDING,
PUBLIC PERFORMANCE AND BROADCASTING
PROHIBITED. MADE IN GERMANY. GEMA.

0257 ▶ karlssonwilker inc., USA

SKÚLI SVERRISSON
SERÍA

0258 ▶ karlssonwilker inc., USA

Ólöf Arnalds
Hildur Guðnadóttir
Anthony Burr
Amedeo Pace
Eyvind Kang
Laurie Anderson
Jóhann Jóhannsson
Hilmar Jensson
Peter Scherer
Ted Reichman
Skúli Sverrisson

0259 ▶ karlssonwilker inc., USA

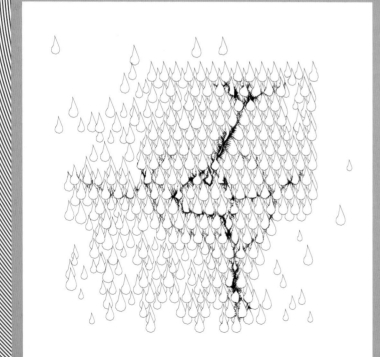

0260 ▶ karlssonwilker inc., USA

0261 ▶ **Ashby Design,** USA

0262 ▶ **Ashby Design,** USA

0263 ▶ **Ashby Design,** USA

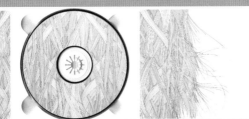

0264 ▶ **Grandpeople,** Norway

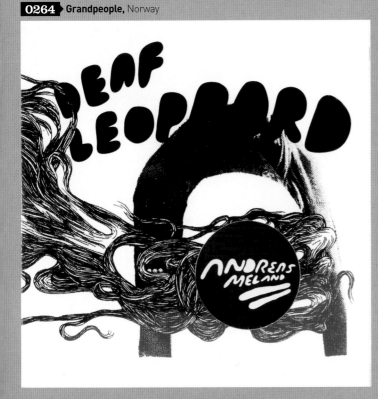

0265 ▶ **Grandpeople,** Norway

0266 ▸ Ashby Design, USA

0267 ▸ Ashby Design, USA

0268 ▸ Ashby Design, USA

0269 ▸ Ashby Design, USA

0270 ▸ Ashby Design, USA

0271 ▸ Ashby Design, USA

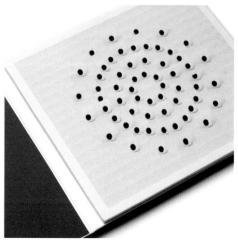

0272 Ashby Design, USA

0273 Ashby Design, USA

0274 T. Lush, USA

0275 ▶ Kellerhouse, Inc., USA

0276 ▶ Kellerhouse, Inc., USA

0277 ▶ Ohio Girl Design, USA

0278 ▶ No Days Off, United Kingdom

0279 **FPM Factor Product GMBH,** Germany

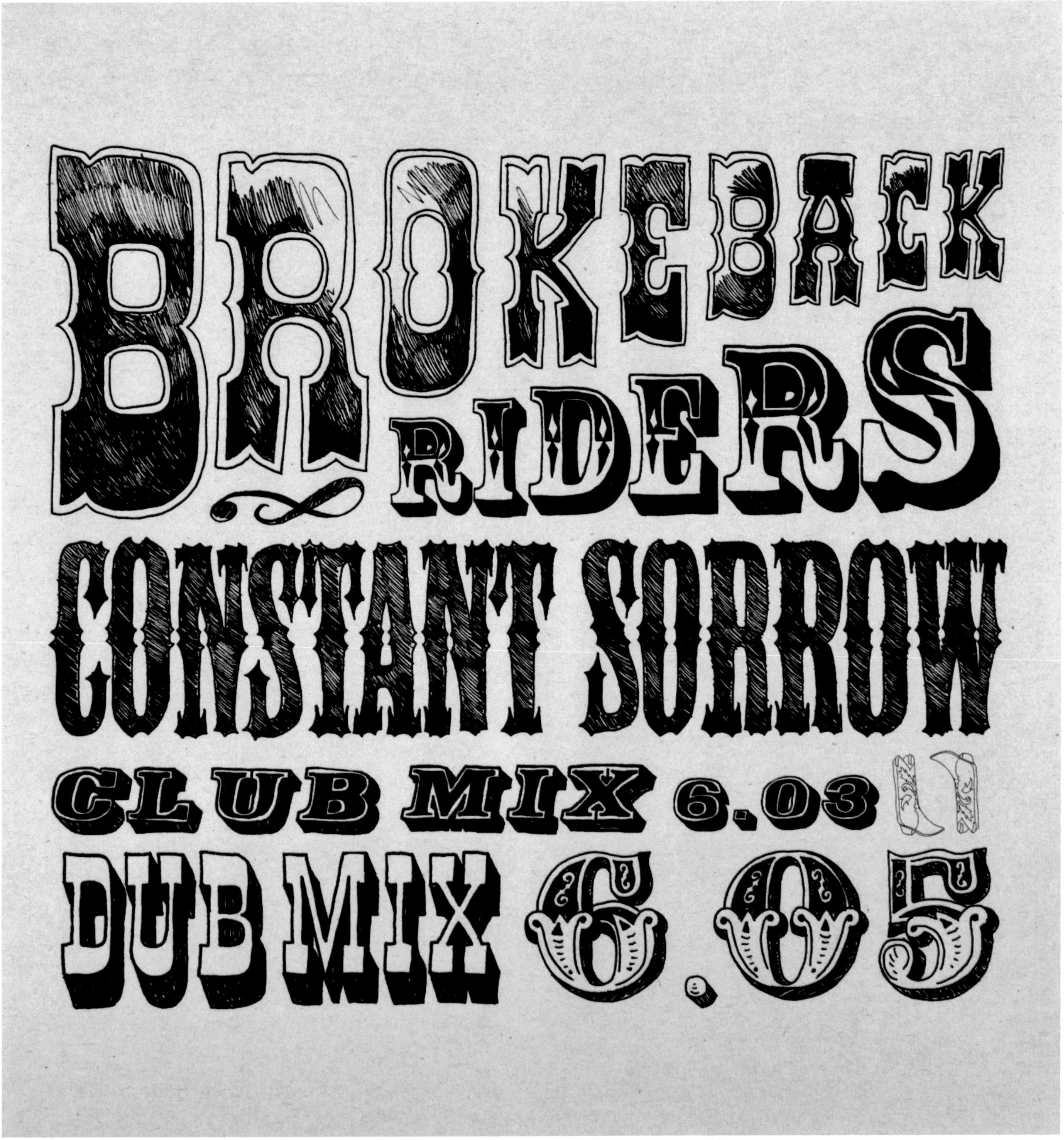

0280 ▶ Kellerhouse, Inc., USA

0281 ▶ Kellerhouse, Inc., USA

0282 ▶ Kellerhouse, Inc., USA

0283 ▶ Kellerhouse, Inc., USA

0284 ▸ Kellerhouse, Inc., USA

0285 ▸ Kellerhouse, Inc., USA

0286 ▸ Kellerhouse, Inc., USA

0287 ▸ Kellerhouse, Inc., USA

0288 ▸ Kellerhouse, Inc., USA

0289 ▸ Kellerhouse, Inc., USA

Jamiroquai

SEVEN DAYS IN SUNNY JUNE

0291 **Yacht Associates,** UK

Jamiroquai
FEELS JUST LIKE IT SHOULD

0292 **Yacht Associates,** UK

Metamatics
MindMushingGit

0293 **Yacht Associates,** UK

Jamiroquai
(DON'T) GIVE HATE A CHANCE

0294 **Yacht Associates,** UK

0295 ▶ Gravillis, Inc., USA

0296 ▶ Gravillis, Inc., USA

0297 ▶ Gravillis, Inc., USA

0298 ▶ Gravillis, Inc., USA

0299 ▶ Gravillis, Inc., USA

0300 ▶ Gravillis, Inc., USA

0301 ▶ **Kinetic Singapore,** Singapore

0302 ▶ **Kinetic Singapore,** Singapore

0303 ▶ **Kinetic Singapore,** Singapore

0304 ▶ **Beggars Group,** USA

0305 ▶ **re-public,** Denmark

0306 ▶ **Timothy O'Donnell,** USA

0307 ▶ Rick Myers, UK

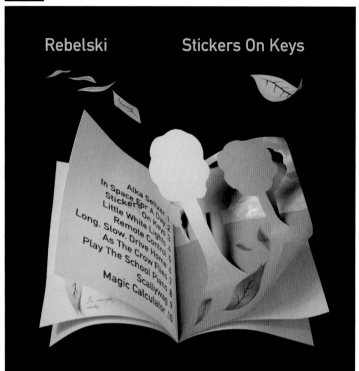

0308 ▶ Rick Myers, UK

0309 ▶ Rick Myers, UK

0310 ▶ Rick Myers, UK

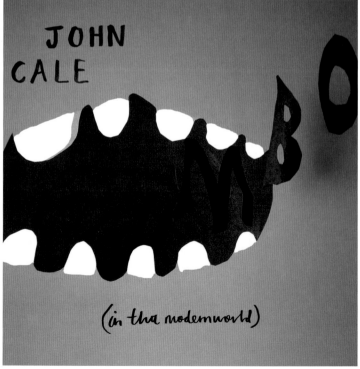

0312 ▶ **This Way Design,** Norway

0313 ▶ **This Way Design,** Norway

BEYOND THE APOCALYPSE
1. Chasing Dragons   2. Beyond The Apocalypse   3. Aiwass Aeon   4. Necronatalenheten
5. Perished in Pain   6. Singer of Strange Songs   7. Blood is the Mortar   8. Internal Winter

EAN 23343993883

0314 ▶ **This Way Design,** Norway

0315 ▶ **This Way Design,** Norway

0318 ▶ **Plazm Media**, USA

0319 ▶ **Plazm Media**, USA

0320 ▶ **Plazm Media**, USA

0321 ▶ **Form**, UK

0322 ▶ karlssonwilker inc., USA

0323 ▶ Plazm Media, USA

0324 ▶ Plazm Media, USA

0325 ▶ Plazm Media, USA

0326 ▶ shed, UK

0327 ▶ shed, UK

0328 ▶ shed, UK

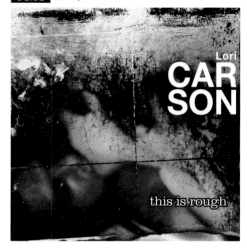

0329 ▶ shed, UK

0330 ▶ shed, UK

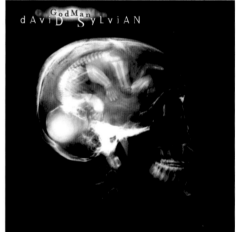

0331 ▶ shed, UK

0332 ▶ shed, UK

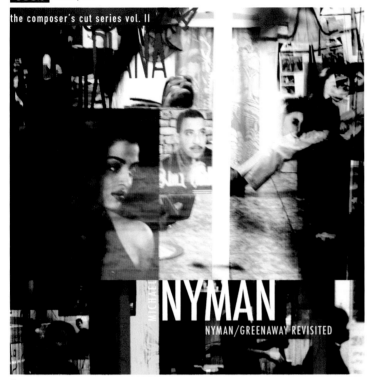

the composer's cut series vol. II

MICHAEL NYMAN

NYMAN/GREENAWAY REVISITED

0333 ▶ shed, UK

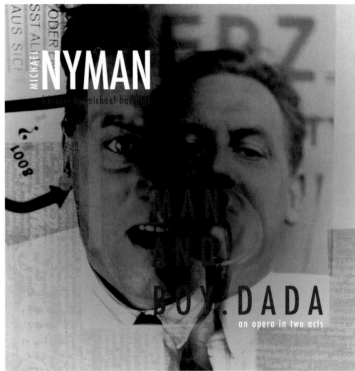

MICHAEL NYMAN

libretto by michael hastings

MAN AND BOY: DADA

an opera in two acts

0334 ▶ shed, UK

MICHAEL NYMAN

THE PIANO SINGS

0335 ▶ shed, UK

the composer's cut series vol. III

MICHAEL NYMAN

THE PIANO

0336 ▶ **Sunto Graphics,** Japan

0337 ▶ **Sunto Graphics,** Japan

0338 ▸ FPM Factor Product GMBH, Germany

0339 ▸ FPM Factor Product GMBH, Germany

millenia **nova** | otra bes

0340 ▸ Kiki Ikura, USA

0341 ▸ Aesthetic Apparatus, USA

HANNE HUKKELBERG RYKESTRASSE 68

0342 ▶ **Grandpeople,** Norway

0343 ▶ **Grandpeople,** Norway

0344 ▶ **Grandpeople,** Norway

0345 ▶ **Grandpeople,** Norway

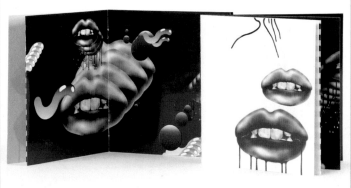

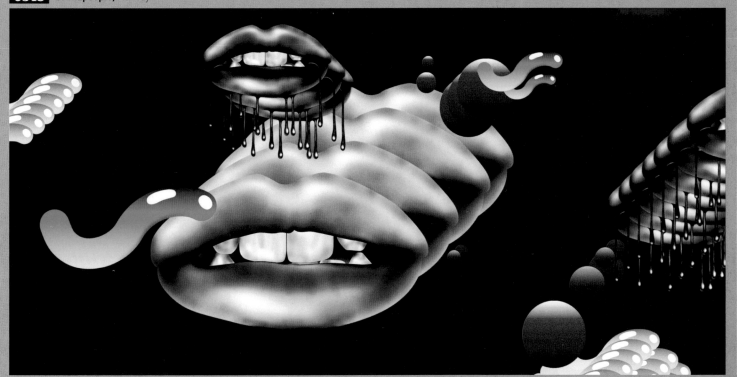

0349 ▸ **Grandpeople,** Norway

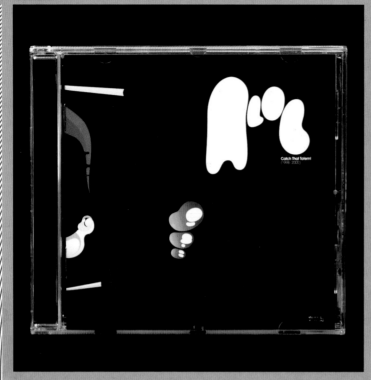

0350 ▸ **Grandpeople,** Norway

0351 ▸ **Grandpeople,** Norway

0352 ▸ **Grandpeople,** Norway

0353 ▶ **Grandpeople,** Norway

0354 ▶ **Grandpeople,** Norway

0355 ▶ **Grandpeople,** Norway

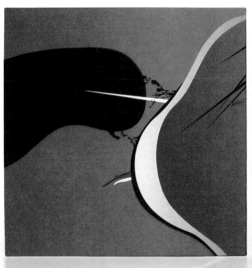

0356 ▸ **Rune Mortensen Design Studio,** Norway

0357 ▸ **Rune Mortensen Design Studio,** Norway

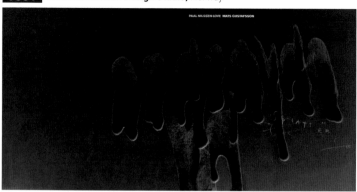

0358 ▸ **Rune Mortensen Design Studio,** Norway

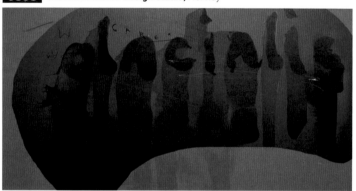

0359 ▸ **Rune Mortensen Design Studio,** Norway

Convertible
'Your Pull Is Gone'

0361 ▶ Sagmeister, Inc., USA

0362 ▶ Sagmeister, Inc., USA

0363 ▶ Sagmeister, Inc., USA

0364 ▶ Sagmeister, Inc., USA

0365 ▶ Sagmeister, Inc., USA

0366 Sagmeister, Inc., USA

0367 Sagmeister, Inc., USA

0368 Sagmeister, Inc., USA

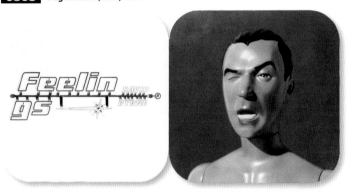

0369 Sagmeister, Inc., USA

0370 Sagmeister, Inc., USA

0371 Sagmeister, Inc., USA

0372 ▶ Sagmeister, Inc., USA

0373 ▶ Sagmeister, Inc., USA

0374 ▶ Sagmeister, Inc., USA

0375 Sagmeister, Inc., USA

0376 Sagmeister, Inc., USA

0377 Sagmeister, Inc., USA

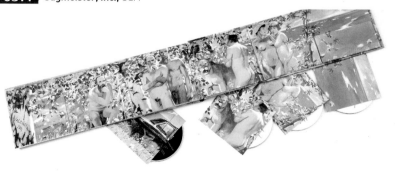

0378 Sagmeister, Inc., USA

0379 ▶ Andersen M. Studio, UK

0380 ▶ Andersen M. Studio, UK

0381 ▶ Andersen M. Studio, UK

0382 ▶ Andersen M. Studio, UK

0383 ▶ Andersen M. Studio, UK

0384 ▶ **Andersen M. Studio,** UK

DISAFFECTED

1. YOU CAN HEAR THE ROOM (06:19) 2. LOVE & MUSIC (04:47) 3. NIGHT OF THE HUNTER (03:12) 4. DISAFFECTED (07:14) 5. YOUR GHOST (06:31) 6. THEORY OF GHOSTS (03:58) 7. I MUST LEAVE LONDON (03:04) 8. DELETED SCENES (01:57) 9. THE MOSTALGIST (03:54) 10. YOU CAN NEVER GET LOST (WHEN YOU'VE NOWHERE TO GO) (04:16) 11. DELETED SCENES (EXTENDED MIX EXCLUSIVE TO SARA) (08:08)

0385 ▶ **Andersen M. Studio,** UK

PIANO MAGIC

SON OF MAR (MUSIC FROM THE FILM BY BIGAS LUNA)

0386 ▶ **Andersen M. Studio,** UK

0387 ▶ **Andersen M. Studio,** UK

ENJOY YOUR PARROT

1. ECHOES THAT DRAWS PICTURES   2. OIL SLIT   3. MONSTERS OF MILLIONS OF PEOPLE
4. MUMMING, HOWLING AND HOODELING   5. PROCESS OF MAKING A PENCIL
6. I SEE JESUS CHRIST   7. THINGS FROM THE WIND (LIVING DREAM OF MIDGET FISH)
8. IT GIVES ME FAITH YOU SITTING NEXT TO ME

0388 ▶ **Andersen M. Studio,** UK

ENJOY YOUR PARROT

1. FORWARD BACKWARD   2. COLOURS OF FORM   3. PRIEST WITH BRUISED KNEES
4. ICH WARTE FÜR DICH   5. TRAGIC STORY OF HOLY LAND   6. ANGER FLOWING IN ME NOW
7. IMAGINARY INVALID   8. HOW MAN BEAT PANAMA   9. HUGE CIRCLE
10. MOUNTAINS OF NOON   11. MAGIC OF SNAKE-MAN

0390 ▶ Gary St. Clare, USA

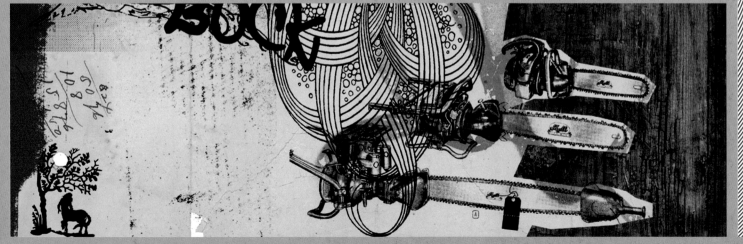

0391 ▶ Gary St. Clare, USA

0392 ▶ Gary St. Clare, USA

0393 ▶ Gary St. Clare, USA

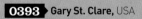

0394 Skouras Design, Inc., USA

0395 Skouras Design, Inc., USA

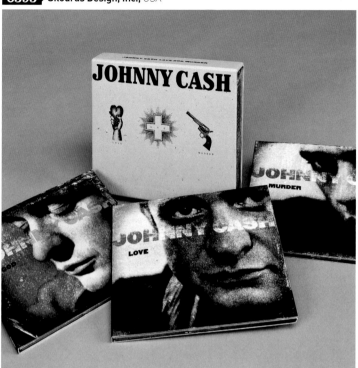

0396 Skouras Design, Inc., USA

0397 EPOS, Inc., USA

0398 ▶ Visual Dialogue, USA

0399 ▶ Visual Dialogue, USA

0400 ▶ Visual Dialogue, USA

0401 ▶ Visual Dialogue, USA

0402 ▶ Visual Dialogue, USA

0403 ▶ SMAY Vision, USA

0404 ▶ Tornado Design, USA

0405 ▶ Tornado Design, USA

0406 ▶ Tornado Design, USA

0407 ▶ Tornado Design, USA

0408 ▶ Kellerhouse, Inc., USA

0409 ▶ Kellerhouse, Inc., USA

0410 ▶ Kellerhouse, Inc., USA

0411 ▶ Stoltze Design, USA

Hoyt Axton • The Brothers Four • The Carter Family • Johnny Cash
The Chad Mitchell Trio • Judy Collins • Bob Gibson • Ian & Sylvia
Joe & Eddie • The Limeliters • Trini Lopez • Miriam Makeba
The New Christy Minstrels • Jimmie Rodgers • The Serendipity Singers
The Simon Sisters • And more!

the best of

HOOTENANNY

0412 ▶ Stoltze Design, USA

the best of

HOOTENANNY 1

0413 ▶ Stoltze Design, USA

the best of

HOOTENANNY 2

0414 ▶ Visual Dialogue, USA

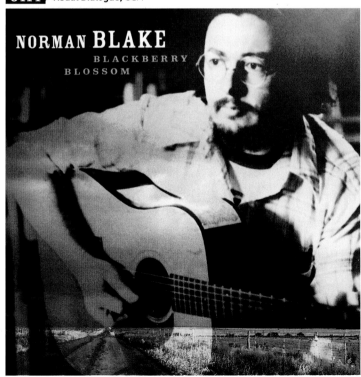

NORMAN BLAKE
BLACKBERRY
BLOSSOM

0415 ▶ Visual Dialogue, USA

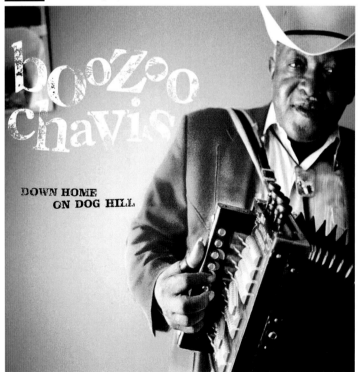

boozoo
Chavis

DOWN HOME
ON DOG HILL

0417 Seripop, Canada

0418 Seripop, Canada

0419 Seripop, Canada

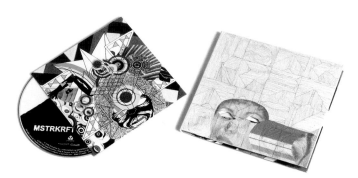

0420 Seripop, Canada

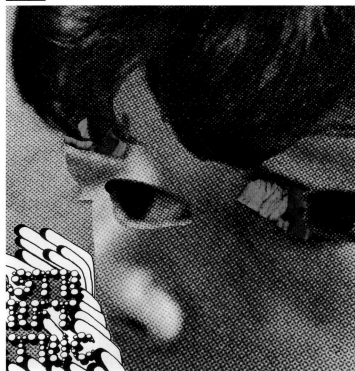

0421 ▸ **Human Empire,** Germany

0422 ▸ **Human Empire,** Germany

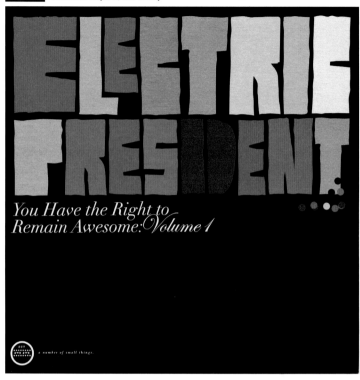

0423 ▸ **Human Empire,** Germany

0424 ▸ **Human Empire,** Germany

0426 ▶ Tait Hawes

0427 ▶ Gary St. Clare, USA

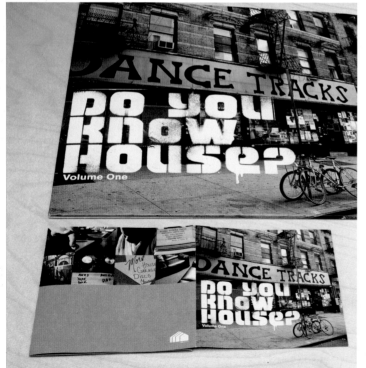

0428 ▶ Subplot Design, Inc., Canada

0429 ▶ Gravillis, Inc., USA

0430 ▶ Stoltze Design, USA

0431 ▶ Kellerhouse, Inc., USA

0432 ▶ Sunto Graphics, Japan

0433 ▶ Adam & Co., USA

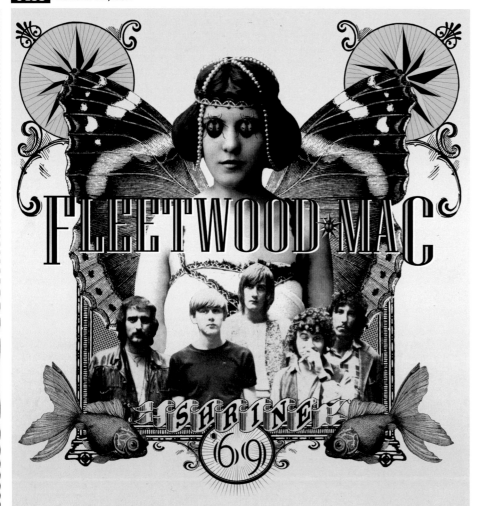

0434 ▶ Adam & Co., USA

0435 ▶ Adam & Co., USA

0436 ▶ The Decoder Ring, USA

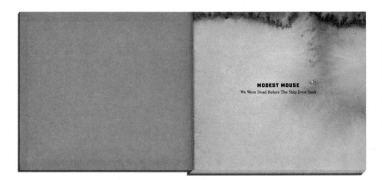

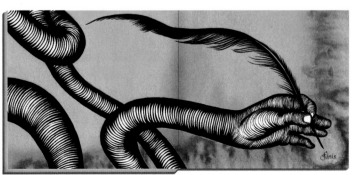

THE ETERNALS

0441 ▶ Licher Art & Design, USA

0442 ▶ Licher Art & Design, USA

0443 ▶ Licher Art & Design, USA

0444 ▶ **GDC,** Australia

0445 ▶ **GDC,** Australia

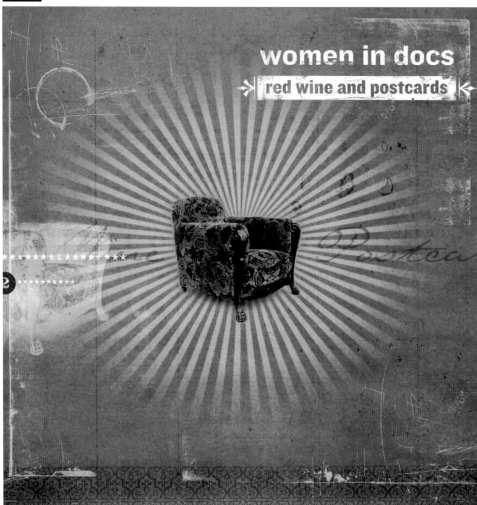

0446 ▶ **GDC,** Australia

0447 ▶ **Teenbeat Graphica,** USA

0448 ▶ **House of Graphics,** USA

0449 ▶ **House of Graphics,** USA

0450 ▶ desres design group, Germany

0451 ▶ DJG Design, USA

0452 ▶ Earwig Studio, USA

0453 ▶ Teenbeat Graphica, USA

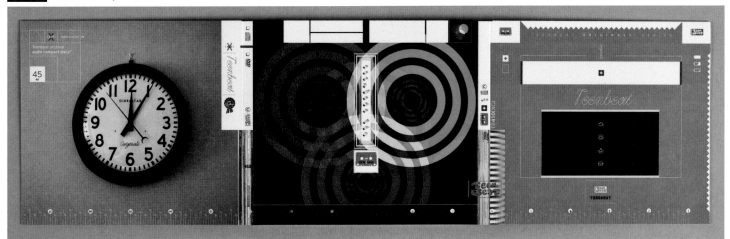

0454 ▶ Soap Design Co., USA

0455 ▶ Soap Design Co., USA

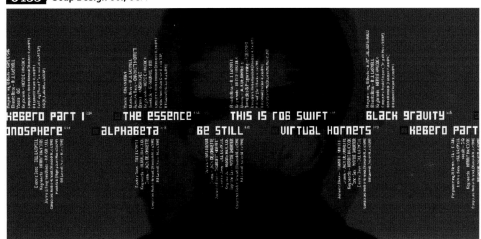

0456 ▶ Form, UK

Younger Younger 28's
Soap

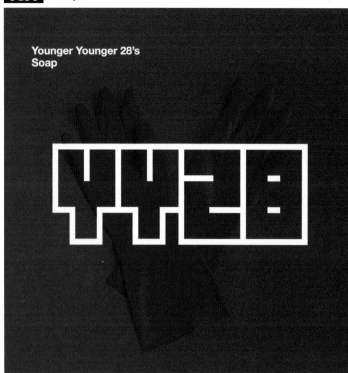

0457 ▶ Form, UK

Younger Younger 28's
Next Big Thing

0458 ▶ Form, UK

Younger Younger 28's
Next Big Thing

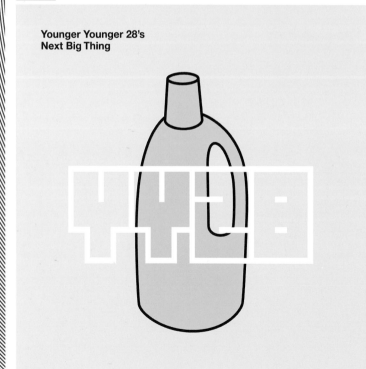

0459 ▶ Form, UK

Younger Younger 28's
We're Going Out

0460 ▶ Form, UK

Younger Younger 28's
We're Going Out

0461 ▶ Form, UK

Younger Younger 28's
Next Big Thing

0462 ▶ Form, UK

Younger Younger 28's
Sugar Sweet Dreams

0463 ▶ Form, UK

Younger Younger 28's
We're Going Out

0464 ▸ **Segura, Inc.,** USA

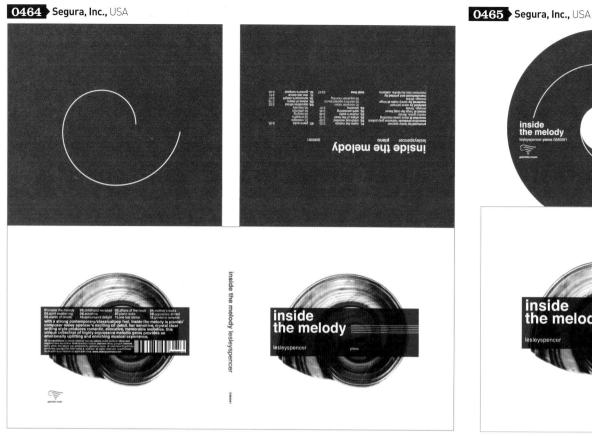

0465 ▸ **Segura, Inc.,** USA

0466 ▸ **Yacht Associates,** UK

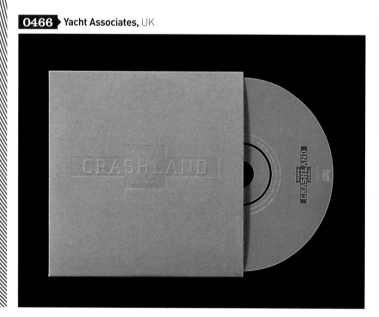

0467 ▸ **Yacht Associates,** UK

0468 ▶ **Beggars Group,** USA

0469 ▶ **Beggars Group,** USA

0470 ▶ **Beggars Group,** USA

0471 ▶ **Beggars Group,** USA

0473 ▶ **Beggars Group,** USA

0475 ▶ **Beggars Group,** USA

0472 ▶ **Beggars Group,** USA

0474 ▶ **Beggars Group,** USA

0476 ▶ **Angela Lorenz,** Germany

0477 ▶ **Angela Lorenz,** Germany

BERLIN

A1 FRIEDRICHSHAIN MIX BY BORIS OF BERLIN / MIXED AND PRODUCED BY B. DOLINSKI PROGRAMMING D. WANG / A2 BERLIN ROCKS ORIGINAL PRODUCED BY ADRIEN WALTER MOHINI GEISWEILLER JUSTE F. // B1 CAN WORK OUT MIX BY SAMMY DEE / EDITED AND ARRANGED BY SAMMY DEE / B2 WIGHNOMY'S BERLIN.JENA.JENA.BERLIN.ROKKER ER.EN.IX / PRODUCED BY GABOR SCHABLITZKI FOR WIGHNOMY BROS. PRODUCTION

REMIXES BY
WIGHNOMY BROTHERS
SAMMY DEE
BORIS OF BERLIN

ALL TRACKS WRITTEN AND COMPOSED BY ADRIEN WALTER MOHINI GEISWEILLER AND JUSTE F. / WWW.SEXINDALLAS.NET // MANAGEMENT REZA DAVOUDI AT ENTHY I / WWW.ENTHY1.COM / MASTERING EGO AT DUBPLATES AND MASTERING BERLIN / PHOTOGRAPHY HADLEY HUDSON WWW.HADLEYHUDSON.COM / SLEEVE ALORENZ BERLIN AND RÄTTVIK // MANUFACTURING HANDLE WITH CARE // WWW.HANDLEWITHCARE.DE

KY04003 PIAS 247.0083.130 FILE UNDER TECHNO / ELEKTRO
P AND C KITTY-YO 2004 WWW.KITTY-YO.COM INFO@KITTY-YO.COM TEL 4910130.4172 80-0 FAX 4910130.4172 80-2
GREIFSWALDER STR 29 10405 BERLIN GERMANY / LC 02016 GEMA MADE IN GERMANY // DISTRIBUTION PIAS NON XEUTOX

ROCKS

0478 ▶ **Angela Lorenz,** Germany

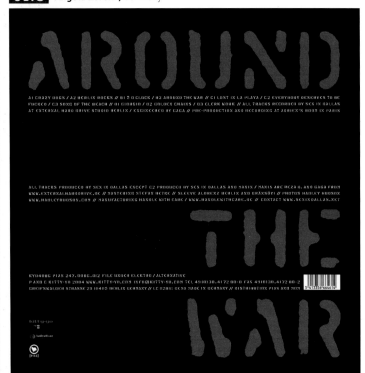

AROUND

A1 CRAZY DOGS / A2 BERLIN ROCKS // B1 5 O CLOCK / B2 AROUND THE WAR / C1 LOST IN LA PLAYA / C2 EVERYBODY DESERVES TO BE FUCKED / C3 SONG OF THE BEACH / D1 GIORGIO / D2 GOLDEN CHAINS / D3 CLEAR WORK // ALL TRACKS RECORDED BY SEX IN DALLAS AT EXTERNAL HARD DRIVE STUDIO BERLIN / ENGINEERED BY GAGA // PRE-PRODUCTION AND RECORDING AT ADRIEN'S ROOM IN PARIS

ALL TRACKS PRODUCED BY SEX IN DALLAS EXCEPT C2 PRODUCED BY SEX IN DALLAS AND MANIX / MANIX ARE REZA D. AND GAGA FROM WWW.EXTERNALHARDDRIVE.DE // MASTERING STEFAN BETKE // SLEEVE ALORENZ BERLIN AND GRÄNNDVI // PHOTOS HADLEY HUDSON WWW.HADLEYHUDSON.COM // MANUFACTURING HANDLE WITH CARE // WWW.HANDLEWITHCARE.DE // CONTACT WWW.SEXINDALLAS.NET

KY04006 PIAS 247.0086.012 FILE UNDER ELEKTRO / ALTERNATIVE
P AND C KITTY-YO 2004 WWW.KITTY-YO.COM INFO@KITTY-YO.COM TEL 4910130.4172 80-0 FAX 4910130.4172 80-2
GREIFSWALDER STRASSE 29 10405 BERLIN GERMANY / LC 02016 GEMA MADE IN GERMANY // DISTRIBUTION PIAS AND NON

THE
WAR

0479 ▶ **Angela Lorenz,** Germany

SEX
IN
DALLAS

0480 ► Angela Lorenz, *Germany*

0481 ► Angela Lorenz, *Germany*

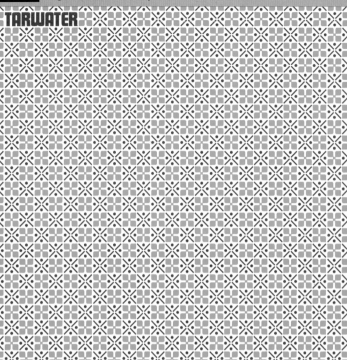

0482 ► Angela Lorenz, *Germany*

0483 ► Angela Lorenz, *Germany*

0485 Stoltze Design, USA

0486 Stoltze Design, USA

0487 ▶ **No Days Off,** UK

PANDIT SHARDA SAHAI | COMPOSITIONS OF BENARES

0488 ▶ **No Days Off,** UK

PANDIT
SHARDA SAHAI

COMPOSITIONS OF BENARES

0489 ▶ **No Days Off,** UK

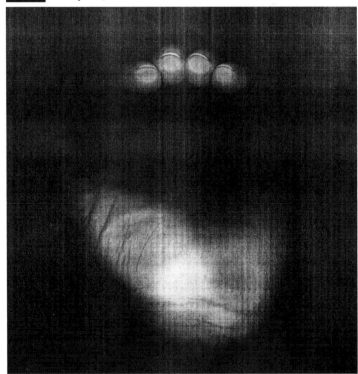

0490 ▶ **No Days Off,** UK

766032 1053-2

1. IMPROVISATION
VILAMBIT LAYA - TEEN TAAL 16 BEAT

2. RARE COMPOSITIONS OF BENARES
MADHAYA LAYA - TEEN TAAL 16 BEAT

©2003 Audiorec Ltd. ℗2003 Audiorec Ltd. Audiorec Classics logo is a trademark of Audiorec Ltd, 21b Si
Centre, 26-28 Wadsworth Road, Perivale, Greenford, Middlesex UB6 7JD, England • Tel: +44 (0)20 8810
Fax: +44 (0)20 8810 7773 • E-mail: info@audiorec.co.uk • Website: www.audiorec.co.uk

0491 ▶ Ohio Girl Design, USA

0492 ▶ Ohio Girl Design, USA

0493 ▶ Ohio Girl Design, USA

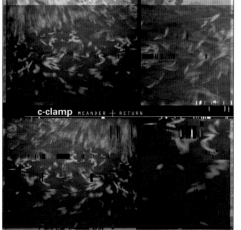

0494 ▶ Ohio Girl Design, USA

0495 ▶ Red Design, UK

0496 ▶ Red Design, UK

0497 ▶ Design by Frank Scheikl, Austria

0498 ▶ Design by Frank Scheikl, Austria

0499 ▶ Timothy O'Donnell, USA

0500 ▶ Timothy O'Donnell, USA

0501 ▶ Timothy O'Donnell, USA

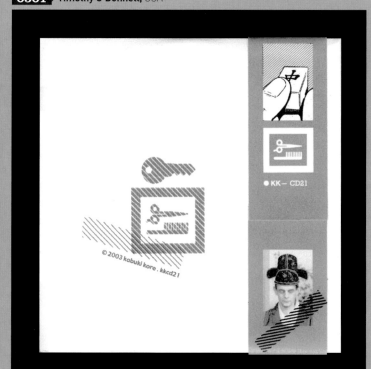

0502 ▶ Timothy O'Donnell, USA

0503 ▸ **Tom Hingston Studio,** UK

0504 ▸ **Tom Hingston Studio,** UK

0505 ▸ **Tom Hingston Studio,** UK

0506 ▶ Mainartery Design, UK

0507 ▶ Mainartery Design, UK

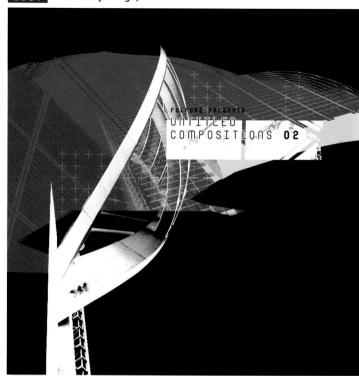

0508 ▶ Mainartery Design, UK

0509 ▶ Uretsky + Co., USA

0510 Power of Beauty Co., Ltd., Japan

御挨拶 メロン完熟

0511 Square Zero, USA

MUSIC OVERHEARD
EDITED BY DAMON KRUKOWSKI

0512 Beggars Group, USA

0513 burofur visuelle gestaltung, Switzerland

blehmuzik

blehmuzik

0514 Gravillis, Inc., USA

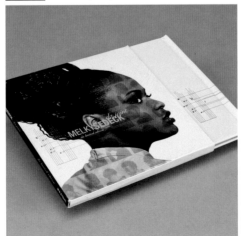

0515 SONY BMG, USA

MILES DAVIS
THE CELLAR DOOR SESSIONS 1970

0516 ▶ Yacht Associates, UK

0517 ▶ Yacht Associates, UK

0518 ▶ Yacht Associates, UK

0519 ▶ Robert Beerman, USA

0520 ▶ FPM Factor Product GMBH, Germany

0521 Teenbeat Graphica, USA

0522 Teenbeat Graphica, USA

0523 Licher Art & Design, USA

0524 Hammerpress, USA

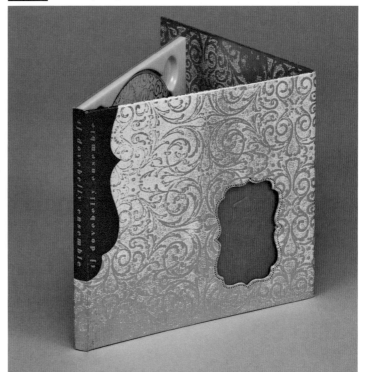

Chapter 2

Posters

Screen printed, digital, hand done, and other works of art

0525-0823

0525 ▸ Aesthetic Apparatus, USA

0526 ▸ Aesthetic Apparatus, USA

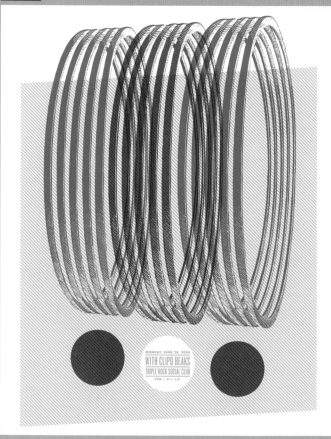

0527 ▸ Aesthetic Apparatus, USA

0528 ▸ Aesthetic Apparatus, USA

0529 ▸ Aesthetic Apparatus, USA

0530 ▶ Aesthetic Apparatus, USA

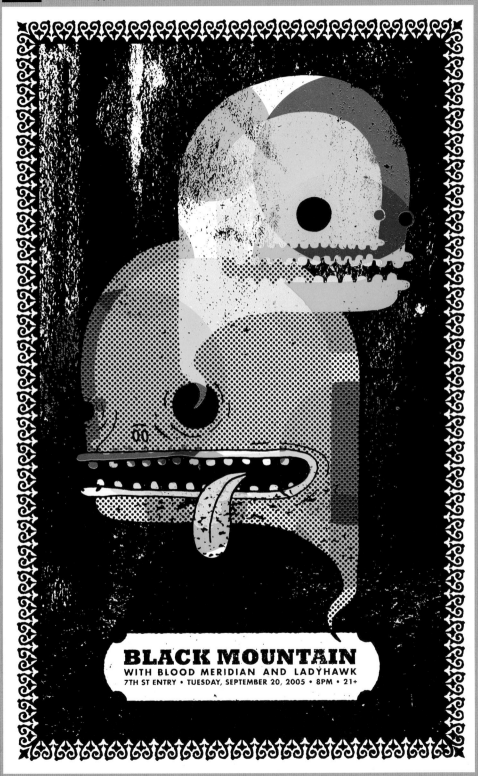

BLACK MOUNTAIN
WITH BLOOD MERIDIAN AND LADYHAWK
7TH ST ENTRY • TUESDAY, SEPTEMBER 20, 2005 • 8PM • 21+

0531 ▶ Aesthetic Apparatus, USA

0532 ▶ Aesthetic Apparatus, USA

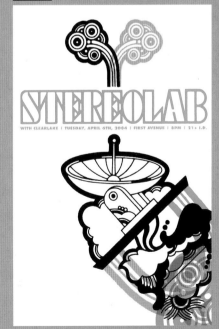

0533 ▶ Aesthetic Apparatus, USA

THE SUBMARINES DECLARE A NEW STATE!

0534 ▶ Aesthetic Apparatus, USA

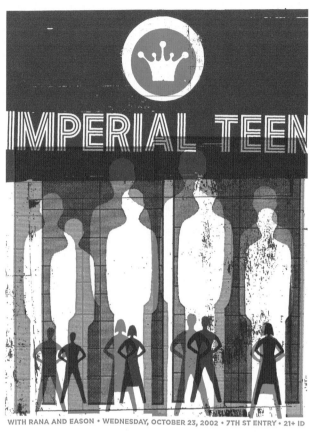

IMPERIAL TEEN

WITH RANA AND EASON • WEDNESDAY, OCTOBER 23, 2002 • 7TH ST ENTRY • 21+ ID

0535 ▶ Aesthetic Apparatus, USA

THE NEW PORNOGRAPHERS
with The Frames // Saturday, February 9 // The Annex

0536 ▶ Aesthetic Apparatus, USA

TV ON THE RADIO

TRIPLE ROCK SOCIAL CLUB
SUNDAY, APRIL 10TH, 2005 | 21+ L.L.

0537 ▶ Aesthetic Apparatus, USA

WITH ODAWAS & WHITE/LIGHT EMPTY BOTTLE MONDAY JULY 11 2005 9:30 FREE

ZELIENOPLE

"INK" RECORD RELEASE SHOW

0539 ▶ Furturtle Show Prints, USA

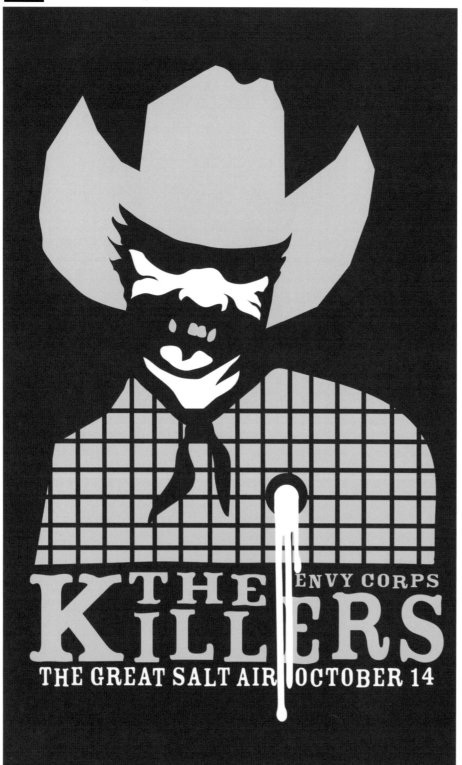

0540 ▶ Furturtle Show Prints, USA

0541 ▶ Furturtle Show Prints, USA

0542 ▶ Miss Amy Jo, USA

0543 ▶ Miss Amy Jo, USA

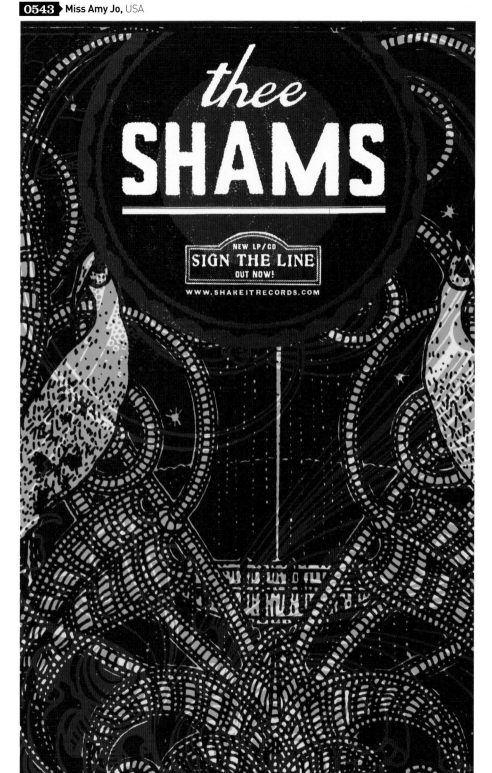

0544 ▶ Miss Amy Jo, USA

0545 ▶ **Art Chantrey Design,** USA

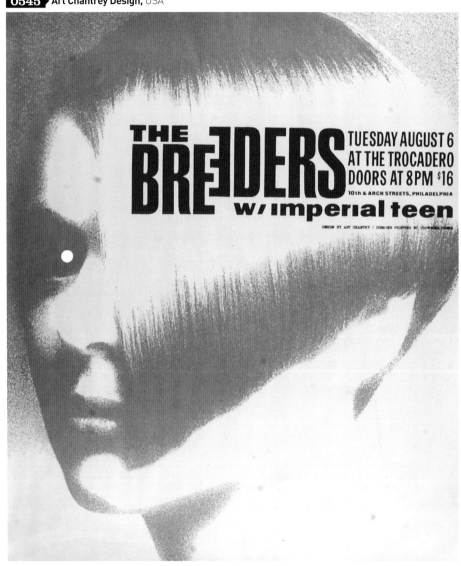

0546 ▶ **Art Chantrey Design,** USA

0547 ▶ **Art Chantrey Design,** USA

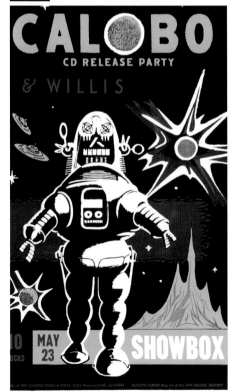

0549 Patent Pending, USA

0550 Patent Pending, USA

0551 Patent Pending, USA

0552 Patent Pending, USA

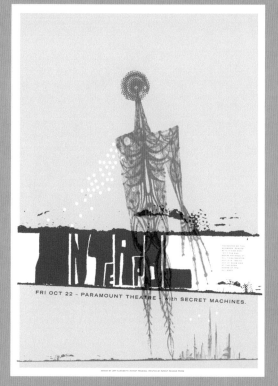

0554 Patent Pending, USA

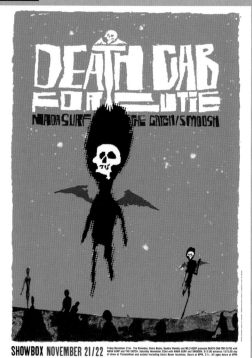

0553 Patent Pending, USA

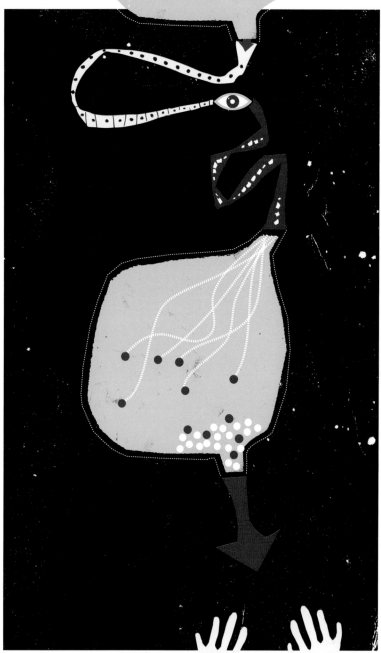

0555 ▶ Patent Pending, USA

0556 ▶ Patent Pending, USA

MONGUI PRESENTS
8:00 PM / $30 ADV / $31.50 DOS

BELLE AND SEBASTIAN

THE NEW PORNOGRAPHERS
PARAMOUNT / MARCH 25

WITH CALEXICO + WHY? JULY 2 SHOWBOX
$15.00 ADV AT TICKETSWEST AND ALL OUTLETS. $15.00 DAY OF SHOW AND AT THE DOOR. DOORS AT 8PM. ALL AGES.

0557 ▶ Patent Pending, USA

WILCO
NEW YORK CITY IRVING PLAZA W / SPECIAL GUESTS JUNE 8, 2004

0558 ▶ Patent Pending, USA

0559 ▶ Patent Pending, USA

0560 ▶ Aesthetic Apparatus, USA

0562 ▶ LeDouxville, USA

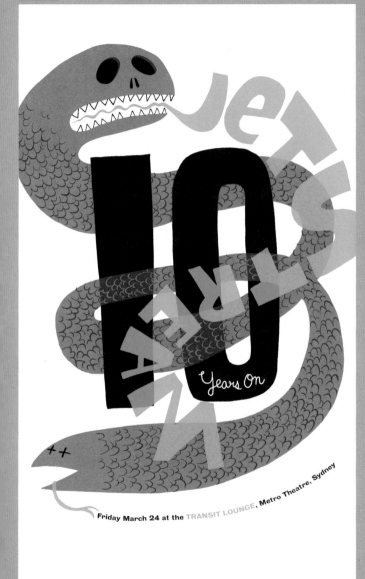

0563 ▶ LeDouxville, USA

0564 ▸ LeDouxville, USA

Presented by
HOUSE OF BLUES CONCERTS and THE SHOWBOX 2

FRIDAY & SATURDAY
NOVEMBER 18 & 19 at 8PM
PARAMOUNT THEATRE
Seattle, WA

with special guest STARS

Tickets are available online at ticketmaster.com,
hob.com, at all Ticketmaster outlets or charge by
phone at (206) 628-0888.

Poster by Jesse LeDoux (Patent Pending).
Printed by Patent Pending Press.

0565 ▸ LeDouxville, USA

0566 ▸ LeDouxville, USA

TUESDAY, MAY 23, 2006 AT THE SHOWBOX THEATER
1426 1st Ave, Seattle, WA · 9pm All Ages · Advance tix from Tickets/West

Design by Jesse LeDoux (Patent Pending). Printed by Patent Pending Press.

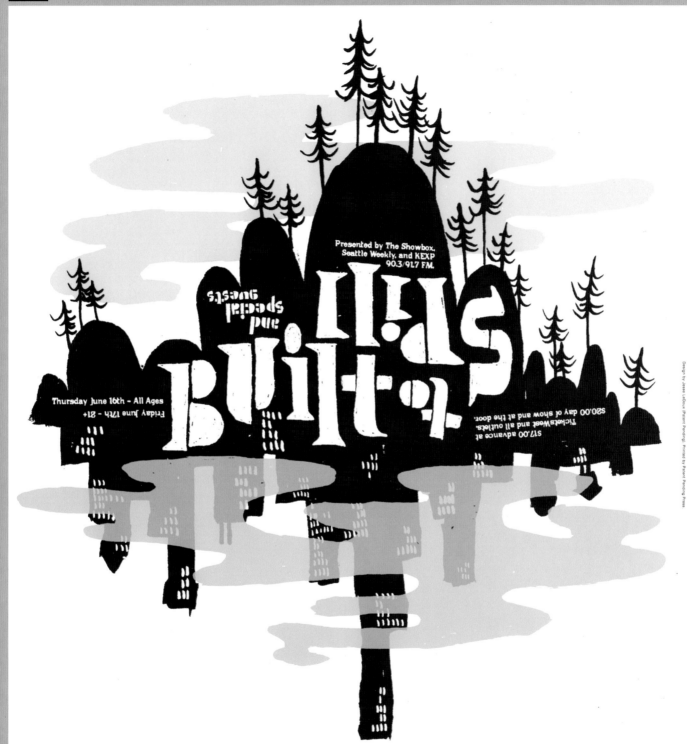

Design by Jesse LeDoux (Patent Pending). Printed by Patent Pending Press.

0568 Dan Stiles, USA

0569 Dan Stiles, USA

0570 Dan Stiles, USA

SHOWBOX SEATTLE
SCISSOR SISTERS
OCTOBER 2 & 3

0571 ▶ Dan Stiles, USA

0572 ▶ Dan Stiles, USA

0573 Dan Stiles, USA

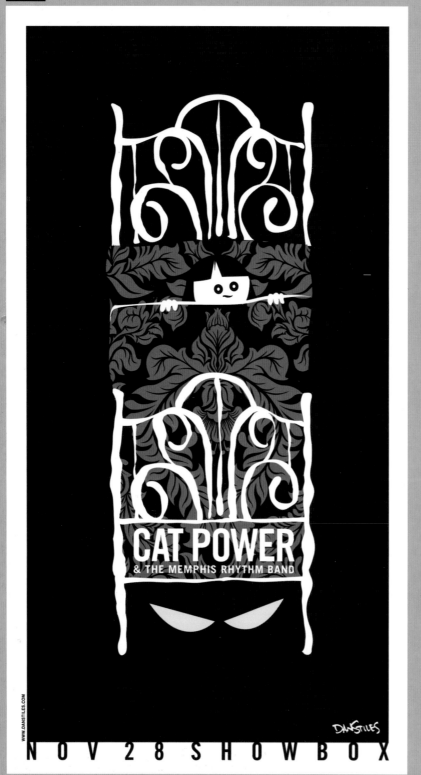

0574 Dan Stiles, USA

0575 Jager DiPaola Kemp Design, USA

0576 ▶ Dan Stiles, USA

0577 ▶ Dan Stiles, USA

0578 ▶ **Hammerpress**, USA

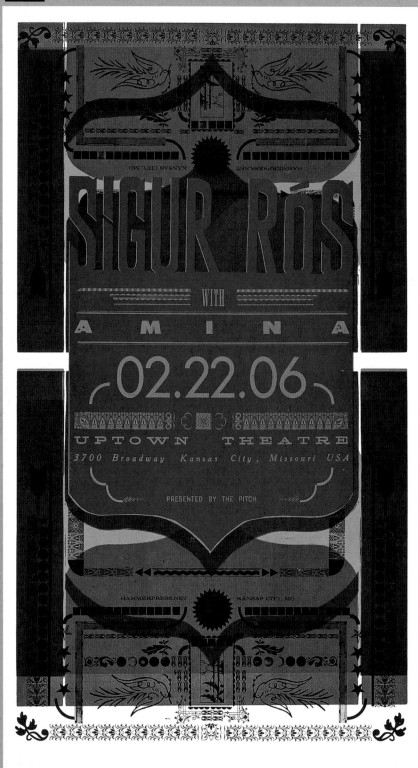

0579 ▶ **Hammerpress**, USA

0580 ▶ **Hammerpress**, USA

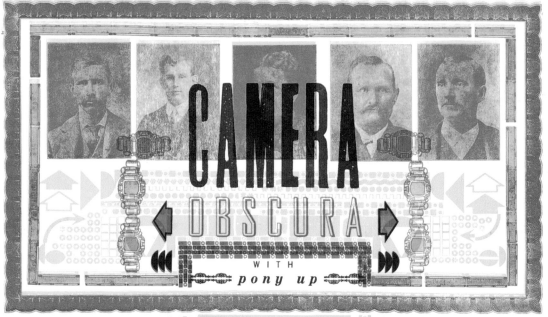

0582 ▶ FarmBarn Art Co., USA

0583 ▶ FarmBarn Art Co., USA

0584 ▶ FarmBarn Art Co., USA

0585 ▸ FarmBarn Art Co., USA

0586 ▸ FarmBarn Art Co., USA

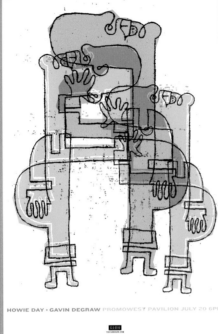

0587 ▸ FarmBarn Art Co., USA

0588 ▸ FarmBarn Art Co., USA

0589 ▸ FarmBarn Art Co., USA

0590 ▸ FarmBarn Art Co., USA

0591 ▶ **FarmBarn Art Co.,** USA

Ryan Adams & The Cardinals ★ PROMOWEST PAVILION ★ MAY 6 2005 ★ COLUMBUS OHIO

0592 ▶ **FarmBarn Art Co.,** USA

0593 ▶ **FarmBarn Art Co.,** USA

0594 ▶ **Douze Studio,** Germany

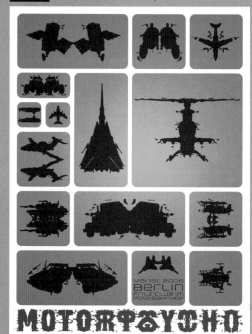

SATURDAY JULY 23 | CASBAH 619·232·HELL

REEVE OLIVER
SATISFACTION
HEDLEY

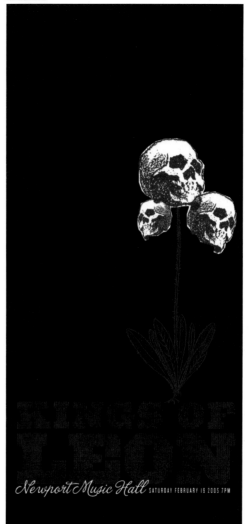

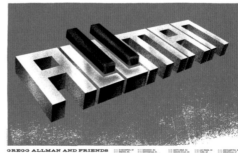

0598 ▶ SRG Design, USA

0599 ▶ SRG Design, USA

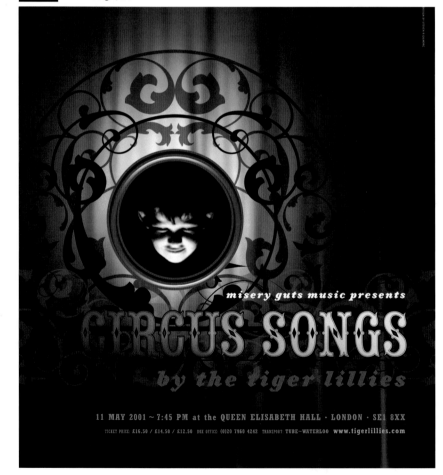

0600 ▶ SRG Design, USA

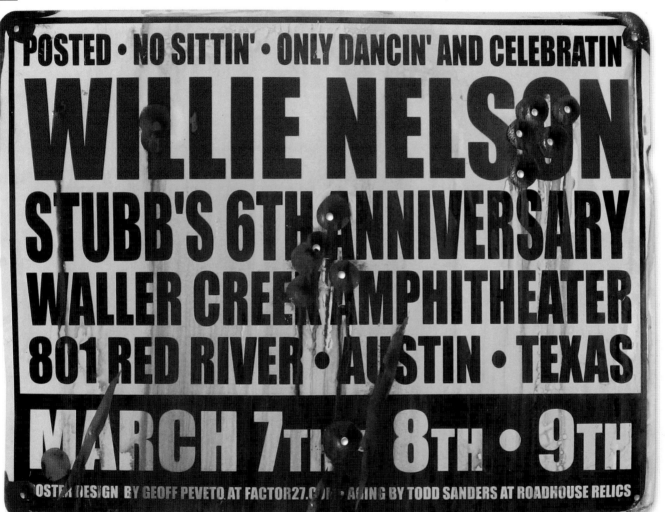

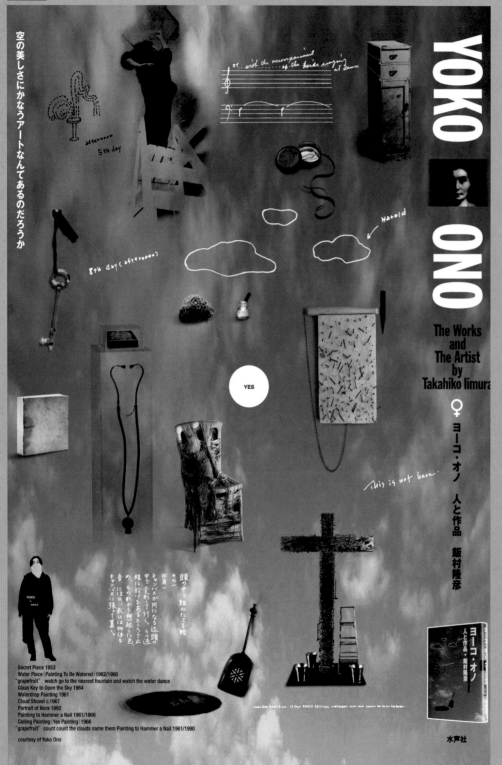

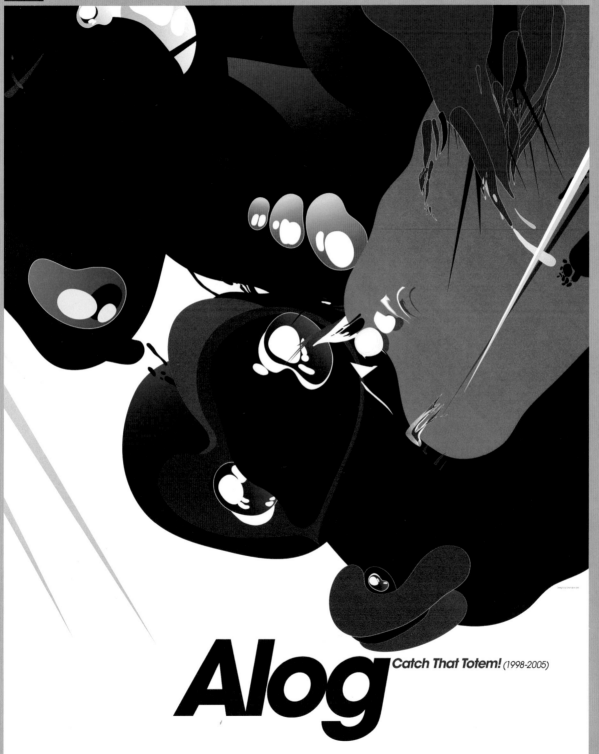

0606 Hatch Show Print, USA

0608 Hatch Show Print, USA

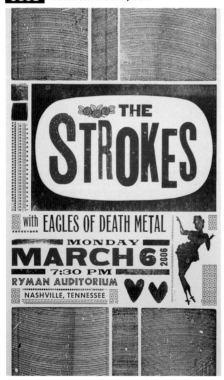

0607 Hatch Show Print, USA

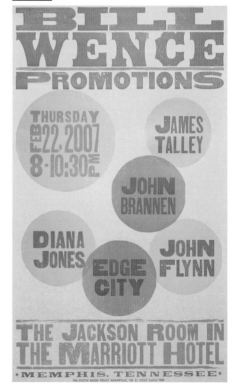

0615 Hatch Show Print, USA

0617 Jon Smith, USA

0616 Jon Smith, USA

0619 ▶ Ames Bros, USA

0620 ▶ Ames Bros, USA

0621 ▶ Ames Bros, USA

0622 ▶ Ames Bros, USA

0623 ▶ Ames Bros, USA

0624 ▶ Ames Bros, USA

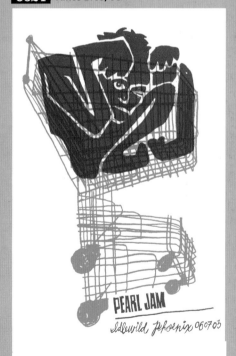

0625 ▸ **Ames Bros,** USA

0626 ▸ **Ames Bros,** USA

0627 ▸ **Ames Bros,** USA

0628 ▶ **Adam & Co.,** USA

0629 ▶ **Adam & Co.,** USA

0630 ▶ **Adam & Co.,** USA

0631 **Adam & Co.,** USA

0632 **Adam & Co.,** USA

0633 **Adam & Co.,** USA

0634 Adam & Co., USA

0635 Adam & Co., USA

0636 Adam & Co., USA

0637 Chen Design Associates, USA

0638 Chen Design Associates, USA

0639 Chen Design Associates, USA

0640 ▶ TEN, USA

0641 ▶ Seattle Show Posters, USA

0642 ▶ TEN, USA

0643 ▶ Fluid, UK

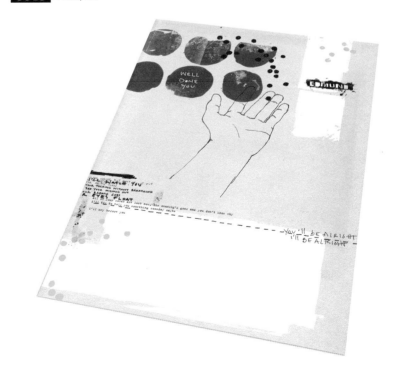

GREAT AMERICAN MUSIC HALL
WITH FOREIGN BORN AND MAZARIN
DECEMBER 18, 2005

0645 The Small Stakes, USA

0646 The Small Stakes, USA

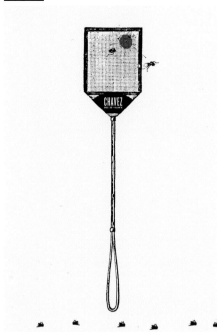

0647 The Small Stakes, USA

0648 The Small Stakes, USA

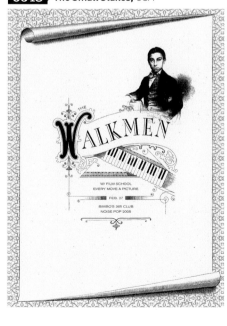

0649 The Small Stakes, USA

0650 The Small Stakes, USA

0651 The Small Stakes, USA

0652 The Small Stakes, USA

0653 The Small Stakes, USA

0654 The Small Stakes, USA

0655 The Small Stakes, USA

ANIMAL COLLECTIVE

WITH OCTIS | GREAT AMERICAN MUSIC HALL | NOVEMBER 21

0657 ▶ Ames Bros, USA

0658 ▶ Ames Bros, USA

0659 ▶ Ames Bros, USA

0666 Jager DiPaola Kemp Design, USA

Thank you **Sonic Youth**.
You made it okay to:

February 18, 2007 with Wooden Wand
Higher Ground, South Burlington, Vermont

0667 Jager DiPaola Kemp Design, USA

Thank you **Sonic Youth**.
You made it okay to:

NOT PLAY SPORTS IN HIGH SCHOOL.

February 18, 2007 with Wooden Wand
Higher Ground, South Burlington, Vermont

0668 Jager DiPaola Kemp Design, USA

0669 Jager DiPaola Kemp Design, USA

0670 ▶ Jager DiPaola Kemp Design, USA

0671 ▶ Jager DiPaola Kemp Design, USA

0672 ▶ Jager DiPaola Kemp Design, USA

0673 ▶ Jager DiPaola Kemp Design, USA

0674 ▶ Jager DiPaola Kemp Design, USA

0675 ▶ Jager DiPaola Kemp Design, USA

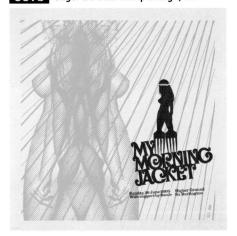

0676 ▶ Jager DiPaola Kemp Design, USA

0677 ▶ Jager DiPaola Kemp Design, USA

0678 ▶ Jager DiPaola Kemp Design, USA

0680 ▶ Methane Studios, Inc., USA

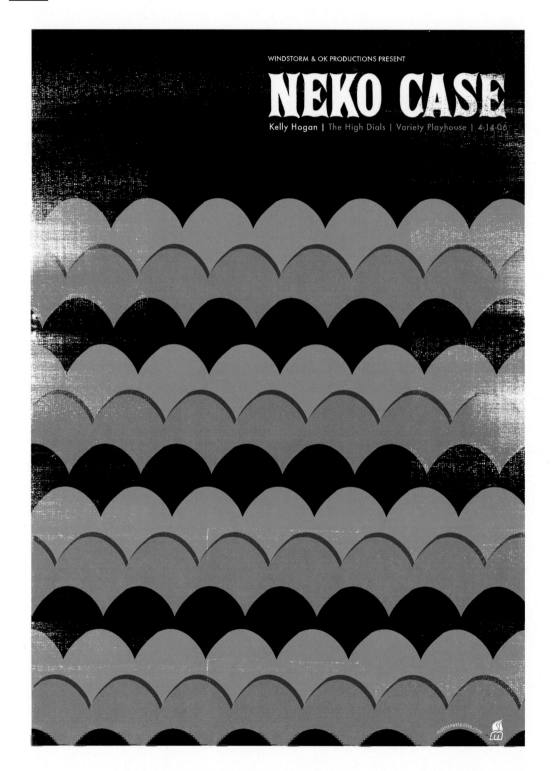

0681 ▶ Methane Studios, Inc., USA

0682 ▶ Methane Studios, Inc., USA

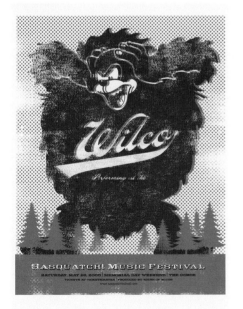

0683 ▶ Methane Studios, Inc., USA

0684 ▶ Methane Studios, Inc., USA

0686 ▶ Aesthetic Apparatus, USA

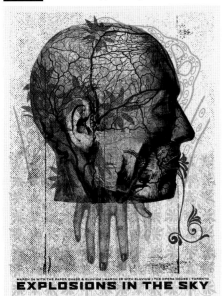

0688 ▶ Aesthetic Apparatus, USA

0687 ▶ Aesthetic Apparatus, USA

0689 ▸ Modern Dog Design Co., USA

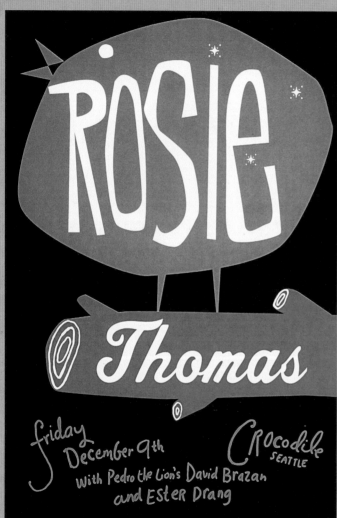

0690 ▸ Modern Dog Design Co., USA

0691 ▶ Modern Dog Design Co., USA

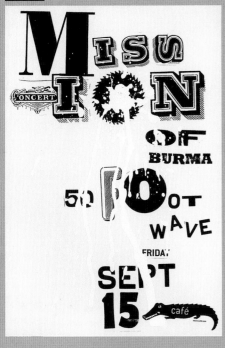

0692 ▶ Modern Dog Design Co., USA

0693 ▶ Modern Dog Design Co., USA

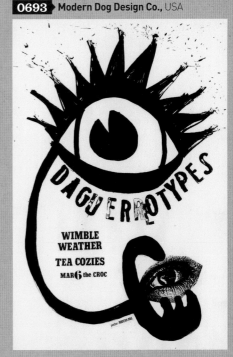

0694 ▶ Modern Dog Design Co., USA

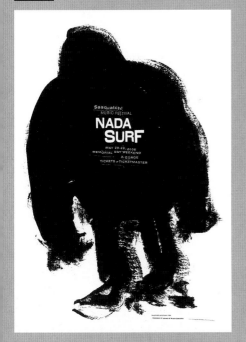

0695 ▶ Modern Dog Design Co., USA

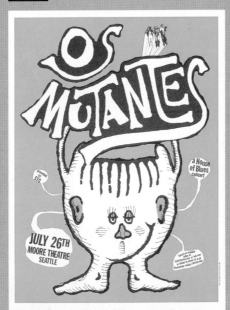

0696 ▶ Modern Dog Design Co., USA

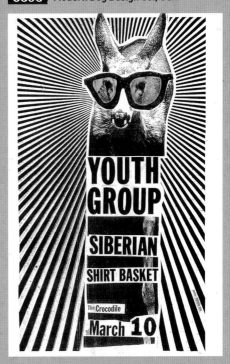

0697 Modern Dog Design Co., USA

0698 Modern Dog Design Co., USA

0699 Modern Dog Design Co., USA

0700 Modern Dog Design Co., USA

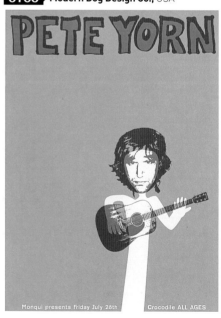

0701 Modern Dog Design Co., USA

0702 Modern Dog Design Co., USA

0703 ▶ Modern Dog Design Co., USA

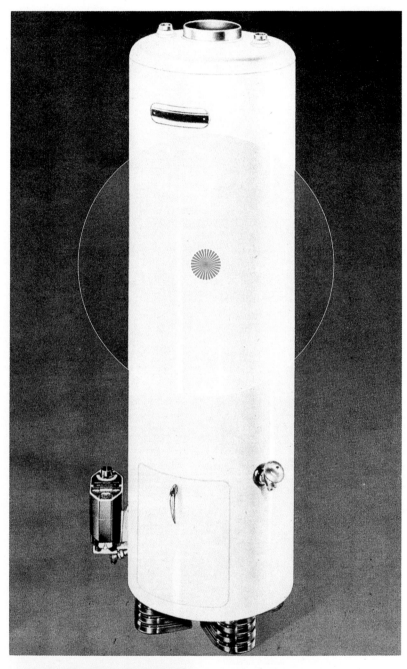

Modest Mouse...................$20
with Special Guest
April 11th, 2004 at the
Paramount Theatre in Seattle
a House of Blues concert
www.Ticketmaster.com

0704 ▶ Modern Dog Design Co., USA

0705 ▶ Modern Dog Design Co., USA

0706 Post Typography, USA

0708 Post Typography, USA

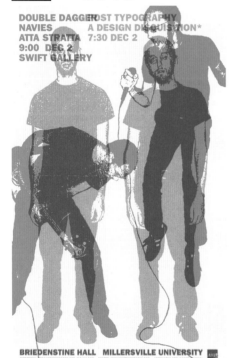

0707 Post Typography, USA

0709 ▸ Post Typography, USA

0710 ▸ Post Typography, USA

0711 ▸ Post Typography, USA

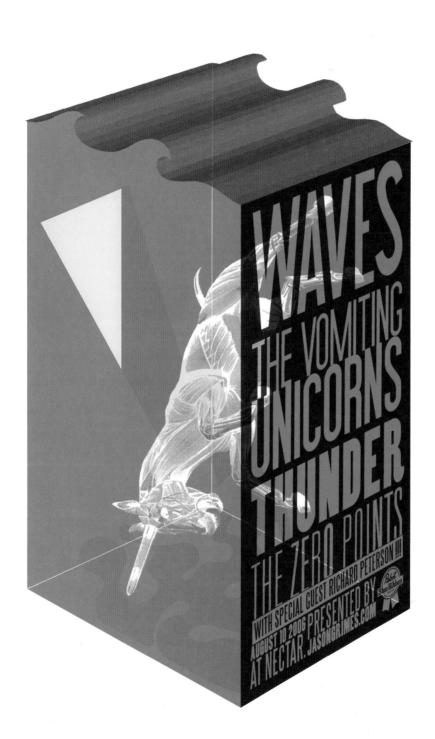

0714 ▶ Jon Smith, USA

0716 ▶ Jon Smith, USA

0715 ▶ Jon Smith, USA

0717 Jon Smith, USA

0718 Jon Smith, USA

0719 Jon Smith, USA

0720 ▶ Jon Smith, USA

0721 ▶ Jon Smith, USA

0722 ▶ Jon Smith, USA

0723 ▶ Jon Smith, USA

0724 ▶ **Seripop,** Canada

0725 ▶ **Seripop,** Canada

0726 ▶ **Seripop,** Canada

0727 ▸ **Seripop,** Canada

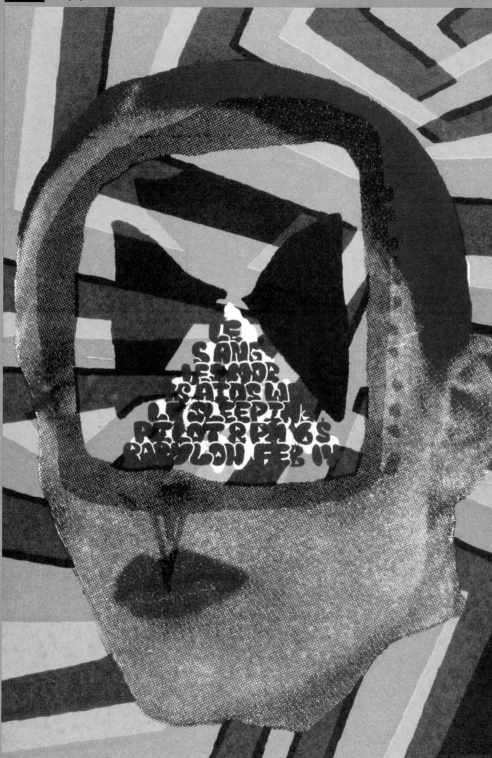

0728 ▸ **Seripop,** Canada

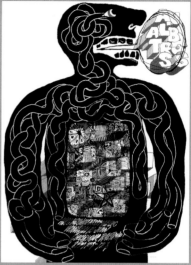

0729 ▸ **Seripop,** Canada

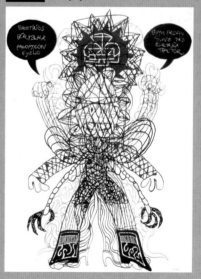

0730 ▶ Segura Inc., USA

0731 ▶ Tim Gough, USA

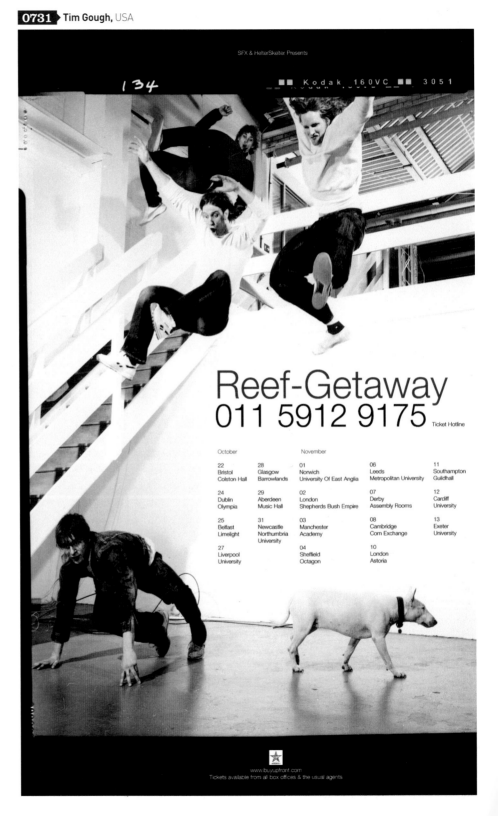

0732 ▸ Spotco, USA

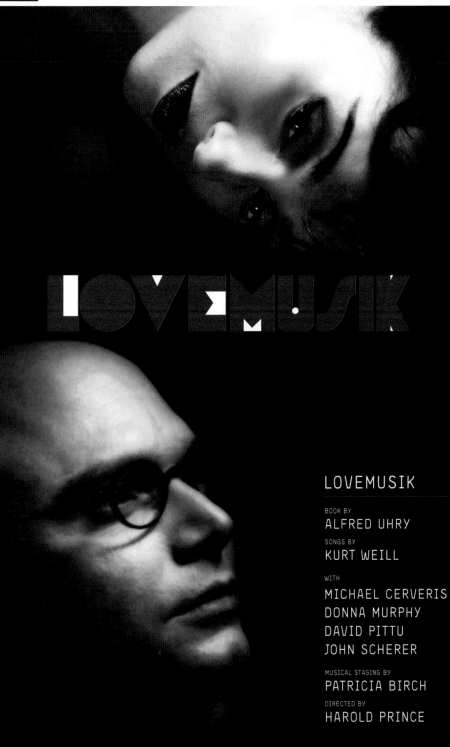

LOVEMUSIK

LOVEMUSIK

BOOK BY
ALFRED UHRY

SONGS BY
KURT WEILL

WITH
MICHAEL CERVERIS
DONNA MURPHY
DAVID PITTU
JOHN SCHERER

MUSICAL STAGING BY
PATRICIA BIRCH

DIRECTED BY
HAROLD PRINCE

0733 ▸ Spotco, USA

0734 ▸ Spotco, USA

0735 ▸ karlssonwilker inc., USA

0736 ▸ karlssonwilker inc., USA

0737 ▸ karlssonwilker inc., USA

0738 ▶ **Four5One°Creative,** Ireland

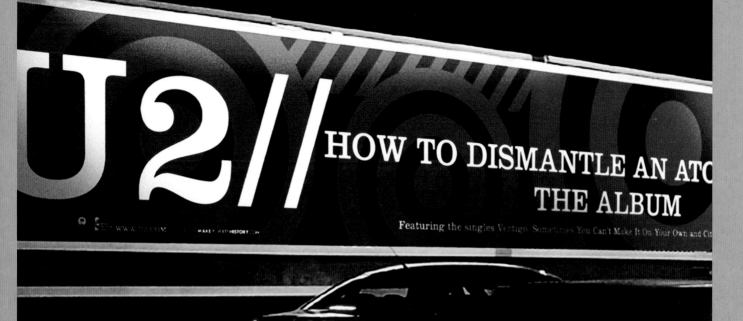

0739 ▶ **Four5One°Creative,** Ireland

0740 ▶ **Tomato Kosir S.P.,** Slovenia

mr★destiny

FRANZ FERDINAND

« Miðasala í verslunum Skífunnar, 12 Tónum og á www.midi.is »

KAPLAKRIKA 2. SEPT.

0742 Jonsson & Lemacks, Iceland

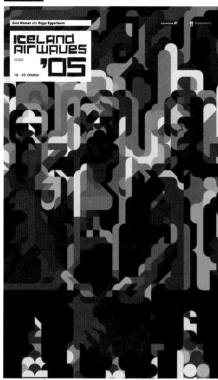

0743 Jonsson & Lemacks, Iceland

0744 Jonsson & Lemacks, Iceland

0745 ▶ Ashby Design, USA

0746 ▶ Ashby Design, USA

0747 ▶ Ashby Design, USA

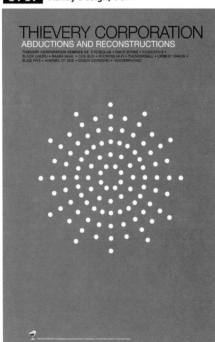

0748 ▶ Me Company LTD, UK

0749 ▶ Me Company LTD, UK

0750 ▶ Me Company LTD, UK

MON JULY 18 2005
FLYWHEEL
$6

RICK MY

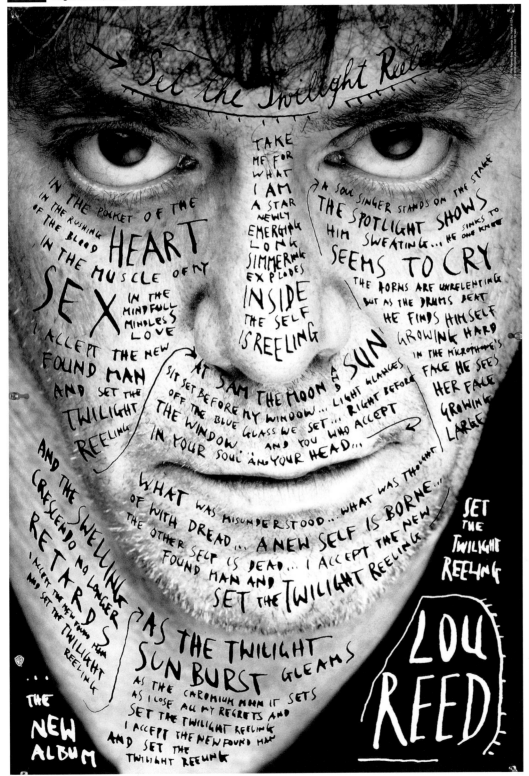

0756 The Decoder Ring, USA

0757 The Decoder Ring, USA

0758 The Decoder Ring, USA

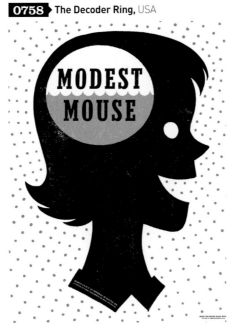

0759 The Decoder Ring, USA

0760 Tim Gough, USA

0761 Tim Gough, USA

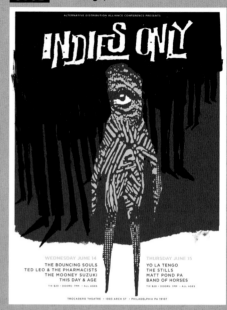

0762 vibranium+co, USA

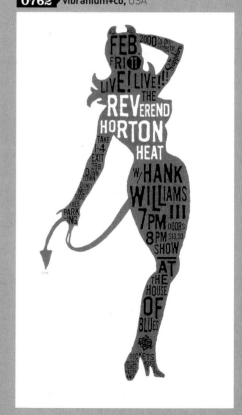

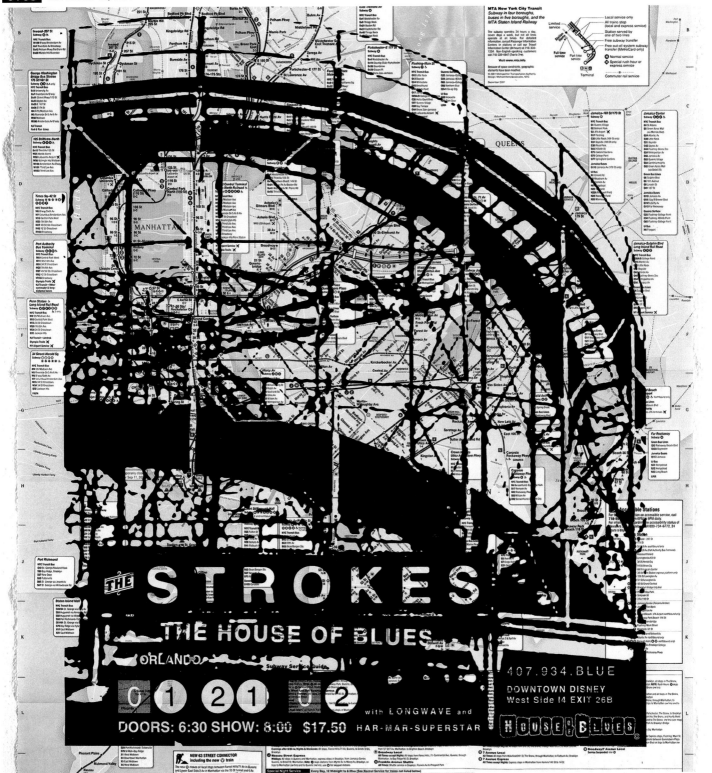

0764 ► Workshop ®, USA

0765 ► Workshop ®, USA

0766 ► Ohio Girl Design, USA

0767 Ohio Girl Design, USA

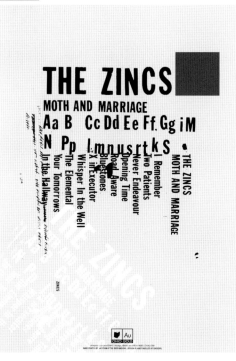

0768 Ohio Girl Design, USA

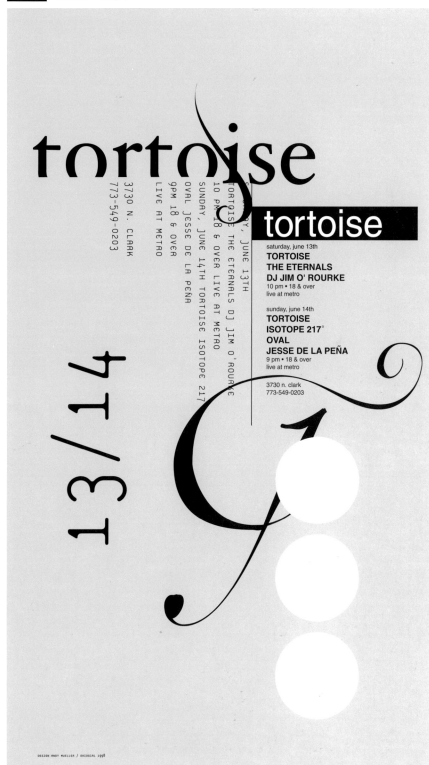

0769 Aesthetic Apparatus, USA

0770 The Small Stakes, USA

0771 The Small Stakes, USA

0772 The Small Stakes, USA

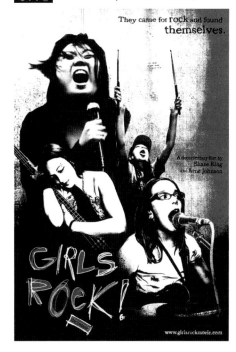

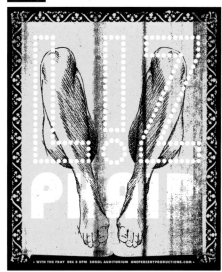

0776 ▶ DJG Design, USA

0777 ▶ DJG Design, USA

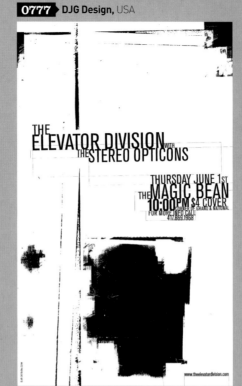

0778 ▶ DJG Design, USA

0779 ▶ Chunklet Graphic Control, USA

0780 ▶ Chunklet Graphic Control, USA

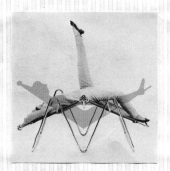

MONTH: WED. FEB. 6

THE PUSH-UP FOR THE MAN

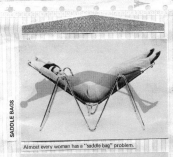

SADDLE BAGS

Almost every woman has a "saddle bag" problem.

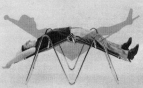

YOU HAVE TO FEEL IT
TO BELIEVE IT!

LAWRENCE KS

BOTTLENECK

NAME: ELEVATOR DIVISION

NAME: ATTENTION

NAME: CLINT K. BAND

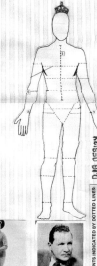

IT
FOLDS
FOR
EASY
STORAGE

FOUNDER

MEASURE AT POINTS INDICATED BY DOTTED LINES   DJG DESIGN
DESIGNED ESPECIALLY FOR YOUR HOME USE.

0782 ▶ **Yokoland,** Norway

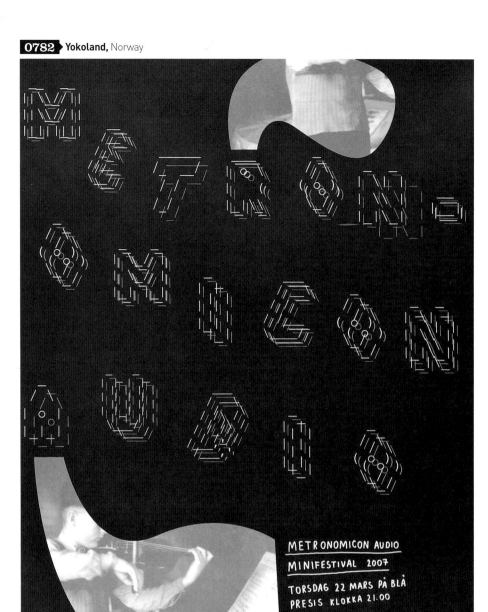

METRONOMICON AUDIO
MINIFESTIVAL 2007

TORSDAG 22 MARS PÅ BLÅ
PRESIS KLOKKA 21.00

LIVE:
NOW WE'VE GOT MEMBERS
HANNY
MAGNUS MORIARTY™
KOPPEN
TRULS AND THE TREES
PILEMIL

DJ'S:
DJ EDB
FRK USB   CC: 100,-

0783 ▶ **Imagehaus,** USA

0784 ▶ **Imagehaus,** USA

0785 ▶ Human Empire, Germany

0786 ▶ Human Empire, Germany

0787 ▶ Post Typography, USA

0788 ▶ Brad Kayal, USA

0789 ▶ Ten, USA

0790 Single Son Studios, UA

0791 Single Son Studios, UA

0792 The New Year, USA

0794 Brian Kroeker, Canada

0793 Brian Kroeker, Canada

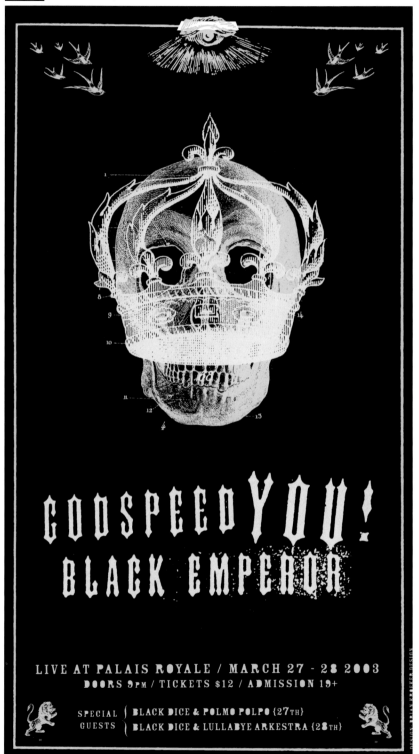

0795 ▶ Hammerpress, USA

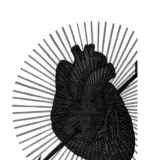

0796 ▶ Melinda Beck, USA

0797 ▶ Switch Creative, USA

0798 ▶ Sidekick, USA

0799 Powerslide Design Co., USA

0800 Powerslide Design Co., USA

0801 Diana Sudyka, USA

0802 Chris Rubino, USA

0803 Diana Sudyka, USA

0805 ▸ **Sidekick,** USA

0806 ▸ **Sidekick,** USA

0807 ▸ **Sidekick,** USA

0808 ▸ **Sidekick,** USA

0809 Sidekick, USA

0810 Sidekick, USA

A BENEFIT FOR THE BEMIS CENTER FOR CONTEMPORARY ARTS
WITH SIMON JOYNER AND THE FALLEN MEN · THE BRUCES · DEC 15 · 8PM · SOKOL AUDITORIUM · 20 DOLLAR DONATION

0811 Sidekick, USA

A BENEFIT FOR THE BEMIS CENTER FOR CONTEMPORARY ARTS
WITH BRIGHT EYES · THE BRUCES · DEC 15 · 8PM · SOKOL AUDITORIUM · 20 DOLLAR DONATION

A BENEFIT FOR THE BEMIS CENTER FOR CONTEMPORARY ARTS
WITH BRIGHT EYES · SIMON JOYNER AND THE FALLEN MEN · DEC 15 · 8PM · SOKOL AUDITORIUM · 20 DOLLAR DONATION

0812 Walse Custon Design, Sweden

0814 Thomas Csano, Canada

0813 Brad Kayal, USA

0815 ▸ Aesthetic Apparatus, USA

0816 ▸ Douze Studio, Germany

0817 ▸ Douze Studio, Germany

0818 Johann A. Gomez, USA

0819 Johann A. Gomez, USA

0820 Jon Smith, USA

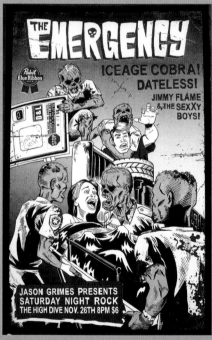

0821 ► **Johann A. Gomez,** USA

0822 ► **Johann A. Gomez,** USA

0823 ► **Johann A. Gomez,** USA

Chapter 3
Paraphernalia

Identities, publications, websites, t-shirts, and other musical matter

0824-1000

P.3

0824 ▶ Bittner Design, USA

0825 ▶ Thielen Designs, Inc., USA

0826 ▶ Grandpeople, Norway

0827 ▶ Ames Bros, USA

0828 ▶ Ames Bros, USA

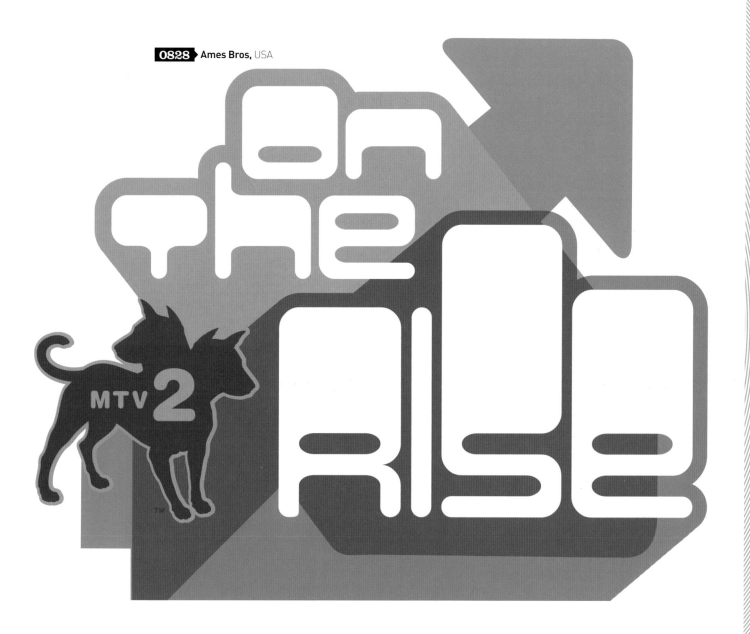

0829 ▶ This Way Design, Norway

0830 ▶ Post Typography, USA

0831 ▶ Sayles Graphic Design, USA

0832 ▶ Judson Design, USA

0833 ▶ Alphabet Arm Design, USA

0834 ▶ Alphabet Arm Design, USA

0835 ▶ Idea 21, USA

0836 ▶ Idea 21, USA

0837 ▶ Thomas Csano, Canada

0838 ▶ Plazm Media, USA

0839 ▶ Johann A. Gomez, USA

0840 ▶ Johann A. Gomez, USA

0841 ▶ Big Active, UK

0842 ▶ Thielen Designs, Inc., USA

0843 ▶ Art Guy Studios, USA

0844 ▶ O!, Iceland

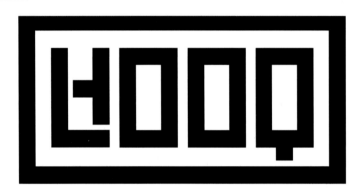

0845 ▶ Fluid, UK

0846 ▶ Gary St. Clare, USA

0847 ▶ Gary St. Clare, USA

0848 ▶ UNIT-Y, USA

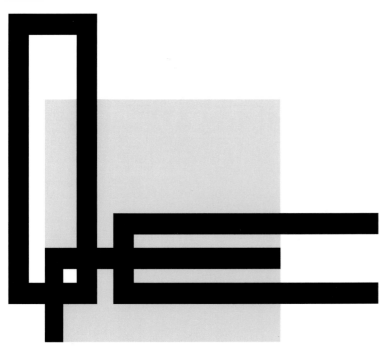

0849 ▶ UNIT-Y, USA

0850 ▶ Gary St. Clare, USA

TOOTS
AND THE MAYTALS
TRUE
LOVE

0851 ▶ UNIT-Y, USA

ALMOSTNØNE

0852 ▶ Gary St. Clare, USA

0853 ▶ Four50ne°Creative, Ireland

0854 ▶ Grady & Metcalf, USA

0855 ▶ Grady & Metcalf, USA

0856 ▶ Grady & Metcalf, USA

0857 ▶ Grady & Metcalf, USA

0858 ▶ Grady & Metcalf, USA

0859 Grady & Metcalf, USA

0860 Grady & Metcalf, USA

0861 Grady & Metcalf, USA

0862 Grady & Metcalf, USA

0863 Grady & Metcalf, USA

0864 ▶ Grady & Metcalf, USA

0865 ▶ Grady & Metcalf, USA

0866 ▶ Grady & Metcalf, USA

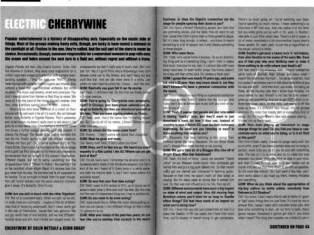

0867 ▶ Grady & Metcalf, USA

0868 ▶ Grady & Metcalf, USA

0869 ▶ Grady & Metcalf, USA

0870 ▶ Grady & Metcalf, USA

0871 ▶ Grady & Metcalf, USA

0872 Go Welsh, USA

0873 Go Welsh, USA

0874 Go Welsh, USA

0875 ▸ Form, UK

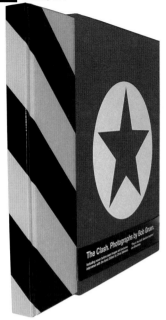

0876 ▸ Form, UK

0877 ▸ Form, UK

0878 ▸ Form, UK

0879 ▸ Ames Bros, USA

0880 ▸ Ames Bros, USA

0881 Four5One°Creative, Ireland

0882 Four5One°Creative, Ireland

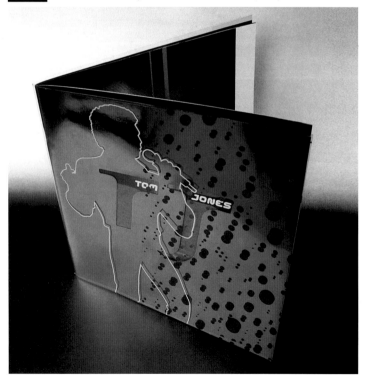

0883 Four5One°Creative, Ireland

0884 ▶ **Four5One°Creative,** Ireland

[*pop for the future*]

0885 ▶ **Four5One°Creative,** Ireland

0886 ▶ **Four5One°Creative,** Ireland

0887 ▶ **Four5One°Creative,** Ireland

0888 ▶ **Four5One°Creative,** Ireland

0889 ▶ **Four5One°Creative,** Ireland

0890 ▶ **Four5One°Creative,** Ireland

0891 ▶ **Four5One°Creative,** Ireland

0892 Four5One°Creative, Ireland

0893 Four5One°Creative, Ireland

0894 Four5One°Creative, Ireland

0895 Four5One°Creative, Ireland

0896 Four5One°Creative, Ireland

0897 ▶ Sagmeister, Inc., USA

0898 ▶ Sagmeister, Inc., USA

0899 ▶ Sagmeister, Inc., USA

0900 ▶ Sagmeister, Inc., USA

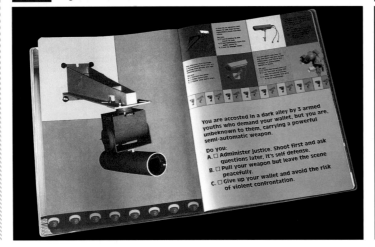

0901 ▶ Sagmeister, Inc., USA

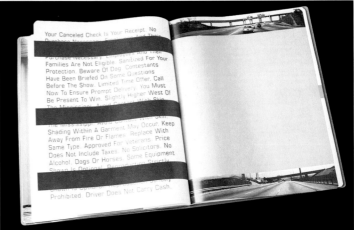

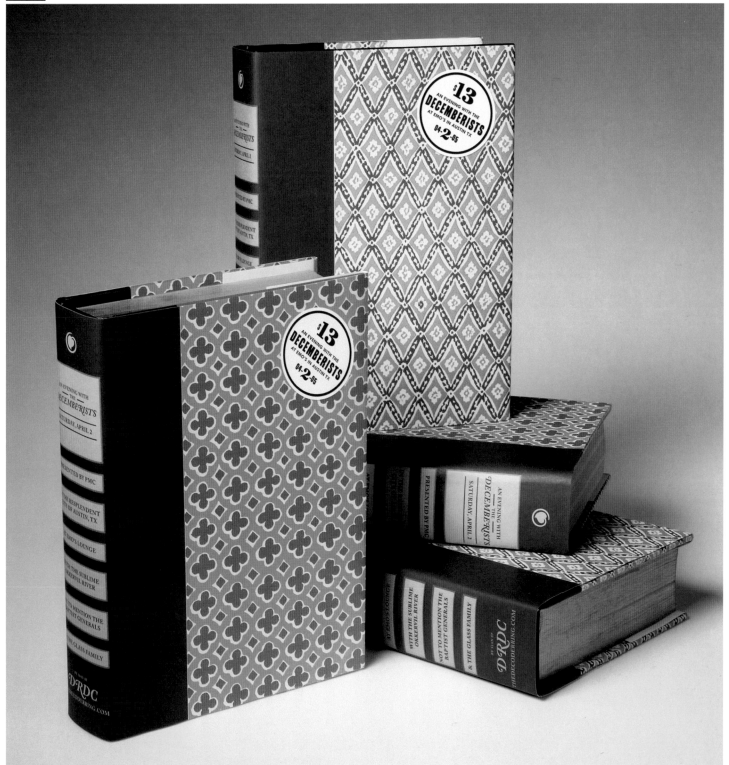

by the editors of
ROLLING STONE

foreword by
**ROSANNE
CASH**

edited by
**JASON
FINE**

**CROWN PUBLISHERS
NEW YORK**

0904 ▶ Spotco, USA

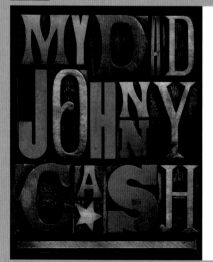

By **ROSANNE CASH**

The summer I was twelve years old, my father
decided that all of us children should learn to water-ski. Every day we started right after breakfast
— me, my three younger sisters, Kathy, Cindy and Tara, and my two stepsisters, Rosey and Carlene
— and we loaded up the boat, which was docked at the bottom of the stone steps
leading down from the home, and headed out onto Old Hickory Lake.

Dad was serene, focused and relentless. He drove the boat to the center
of the lake, tightened our life jackets and sent us each overboard in turns. He
waited until we were in position behind the boat, leaning back in the water,
clutching the rope, skis sticking straight up, then he gunned the engine. He
gunned the engine about a hundred times a day, and some days nobody got up to standing. Most of
the time he had a Coke and a bag of peanuts in his hand, and he absentmindedly dropped peanuts
in his bottle and swigged it all back. When someone finally got up to standing and skied for a few

0905 ▸ Spotco, USA

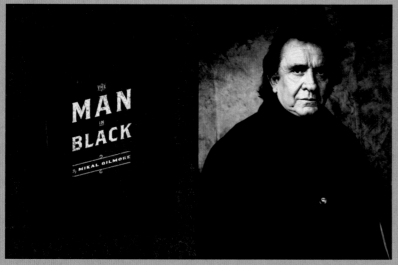

0906 ▸ Spotco, USA

0907 ▶ **This Way Design,** Norway

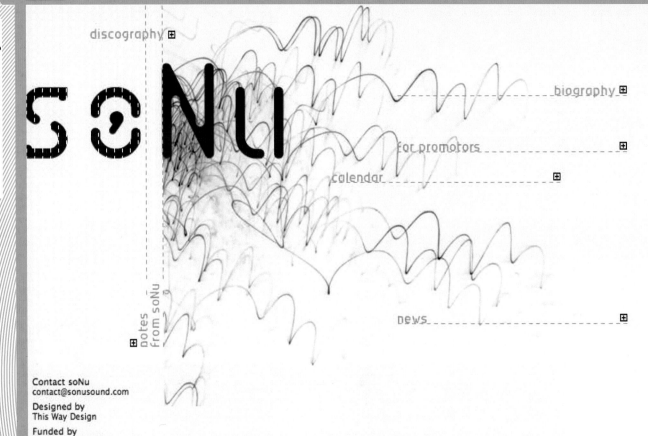

discography ⊞

soNu

biography ⊞

for promotors ⊞

calendar ⊞

notes from soNu ⊞

news ⊞

Contact soNu
contact@sonusound.com

Designed by
This Way Design

Funded by
www.composers.la

0908 ▶ **This Way Design,** Norway

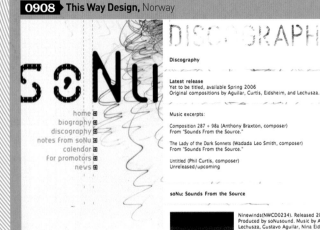

DISCOGRAPHY

Discography

Latest release
Yet to be titled, available Spring 2006
Original compositions by Aguilar, Curtis, Eidsheim, and Lechusza.

Music excerpts:

Composition 287 + 98a (Anthony Braxton, composer)
From "Sounds From the Source."

The Lady of the Dark Sonnets (Wadada Leo Smith, composer)
From "Sounds From the Source."

Untitled (Phil Curtis, composer)
Unreleased/upcoming

soNu: Sounds From the Source

Ninewinds(NWCD0234). Released 2004.
Produced by soNusound. Music by Alan
Lechusza, Gustavo Aguilar, Nina Eidsheim,
Phil Curtis, Vinny Golia, Arash Haile.

soNu

Rex Butters, All About Jazz:
The new Nine Winds release by soNu
presents the eclectic band as a cultural

home ⊞
biography ⊞
discography ⊞
notes from soNu ⊞
calendar ⊞
for promotors ⊞
news ⊞

0909 ▶ **This Way Design,** Norway

PROMOTORS

Promotors

High-res picture for promotors. Click thumbnail to
download.

Download group biography (pdf)
Download individual biographies (pdf)
Download technical info for presenters (pdf)

Said about soNu:

"attractive and surprising, with a convincing feel…"
- The Wire

"Even the oldest pieces performed here still sound strikingly modern,
and soNu drives them without sparing the whip."
-jazzreview.com

"soNu has realized a multi-culti vision rich in texture and imagination."
-allaboutjazz.com

"You would think that a blending of these extreme ideas couldn't work,
but it does work well and doesn't sound forced in any way. This is
another intriguing gem and tasty sonic salad"
-Downtown Music Gallery

home ⊞
biography ⊞
discography ⊞
notes from soNu ⊞
calendar ⊞
for promotors ⊞
news ⊞

THORNS DVD DOLBY DIGITAL 5.1
WARNING: HIGH AND LOW FREQUENCY SOUNDS.
LISTEN WITH CAUTION.

LATEST EVENT

BANKS VIOLETTE:
UNTITLED

Whitney Museum
of American Art

945 Madison Avenue
at 75th Street
New York, NY 10021

May 27 - October 2, 2005
Anne & Joel Ehrenkranz Gallery,
Floor 1

Profile design: superlow.com
Web design: thiswaydesign.com

MELGAARD
KIEL
...

MELGAARD
PARIS
...

VIOLETTE
STUDIO
...

VIOLETTE
NYC
...

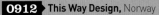

0913 ▶ Edward Mullen Studio, USA

0914 ▶ Edward Mullen Studio, USA

0915 ▶ Edward Mullen Studio, USA

0916 ▶ Edward Mullen Studio, USA

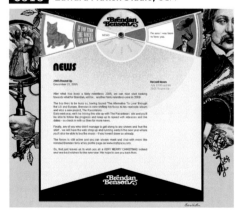

0917 ▶ Edward Mullen Studio, USA

0918 ▶ Edward Mullen Studio, USA

0919 ▶ Edward Mullen Studio, USA

0920 ▶ Edward Mullen Studio, USA

New web site
Friday, October 27, 2006 - This is it!!!

We got a new web site. It is this web site you are looking at. Keep it a secret or too many people will come and clog it up. Same with Gosling's music, keep it a secret too because it is too good to be heard by alot of people. Be different, every one is on myspace, come to this web site to get your information about the world. We will tell you the truth. Look at these graphics!!! These are the high class graphics that only we could afford. You don't need any other friends, music or knowledge besides what is found on this web site. We are also going to spend the money to try to get the squirrel to talk when you put the mouse over it.

News   Gallery   On Tour   Music
Merch   Fan Club   Mailing List   Contact

0922 Toothjuice, USA

0923 Toothjuice, USA

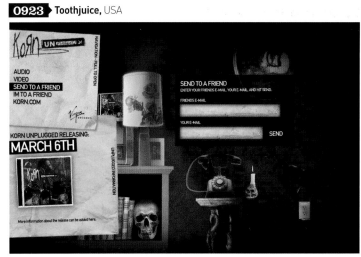

0924 Toothjuice, USA

0925 ▶ Toothjuice, USA

SoThey Say,

Enter the website

Antidote for Irony in stores 3/7/06, click here to order yours today.

Order yours today and get a free poster, sticker, and button from Smart Punk!
Click here to order now.

Featured Links,

myspace
a place for friends purevolume™
WE'RE LISTENING TO YOU!! FEARLESS

0926 ▶ Toothjuice, USA

0927 ▶ Toothjuice, USA

0928 ▶ **Fluid,** UK

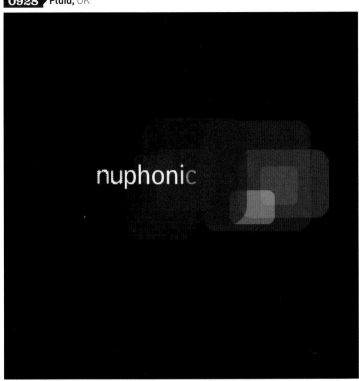

0929 ▶ **Fluid,** UK

0930 ▶ **Fluid,** UK

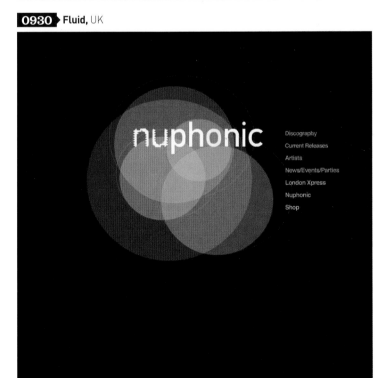

0931 ▶ **Fluid,** UK

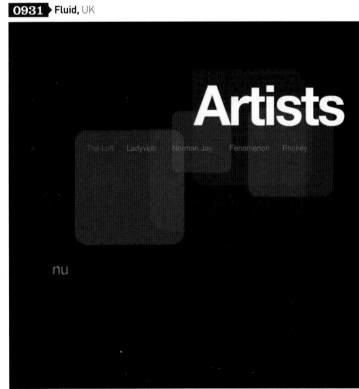

0932 ▶ **Osso Design,** Brazil

0933 ▶ **Osso Design,** Brazil

0934 CandyStations, USA

TORTOISE

CONTACT   WELCOME   HISTORY   DISCOGRAPHY   TOURS   IMAGES   MERCH
                 RADIO   DOWNLOADS   FORUM   LINKS   CASEY'S CORNER

RECORD LABEL

Thrill Jockey Records
http://www.thrilljockey.com/

PRESS

Jamie at Thrill Jockey
jamie@thrilljockey.com
312-492-9634

BOOKING

US:
Tom Windish
http://windishagency.com
tom@windishagency.com

Europe:
Berthold Seliger
http://www.bseliger.de
bs@bseliger.de

MANAGEMENT

Ravenhouse, LTD
http://ravenhouseltd.com
trts_info@ravenhouseltd.com

0935 CandyStations, USA

TORTOISE

DISCOGRAPHY   WELCOME   HISTORY   TOURS   IMAGES   MERCH
                  RADIO   CONTACT   DOWNLOADS   FORUM   LINKS   CASEY'S CORNER

ALBUMS / LPs   albums/LPs • singles/EPs • remixes • compilations

A Lazarus Taxon
Available August 22, 2006

Thrill Jockey, thrill 152

Spanning three CDs and one DVD, this set sums up just about all of Tortoise's extra-curricular activity during their 16-year career, previously only available for two-months-salary prices on eBay. The set is centered around the Rhythms, Resolutions and Clusters LP, which went out of print almost directly upon its release after their first album in 1995, and includes the lost Mike Watt remix track, which arrived too late to be pressed on the LP, and had to be respooled from a broken DAT by Bundy K. Brown just to be included here! The rest of the set is filled out by 7" and 12" EP, compilation, and Japanese bonus tracks. And then there's the DVD, the piece de resistance, as they say. Over two hours long, the disc includes all of Tortoise's music videos; a couple of more conceptual short films using Tortoise's music; and several live sets, including one long set from 1994, and a one-time only live collaboration with Fred Anderson and the Chicago Underground Quartet. The whole thing comes packaged in a striking hard cardstock box, printed with photography by the Swiss photographer Arnold Odermatt.

Click here for more information and complete track listing.
Preorder Available August 1!

The Brave and the Bold
January 24, 2006
Collaboration between Tortoise and Will Oldham

Overcoat Recordings

Songlist:
1. Cravo E Canela   6. Pancho
2. Thunder Road   7. That's Pep
3. It's Expected I'm Gone   8. Some Say (I Got Devil)

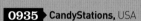

0936 ▶ Kellerhouse, Inc., USA

0937 ▶ Kellerhouse, Inc., USA

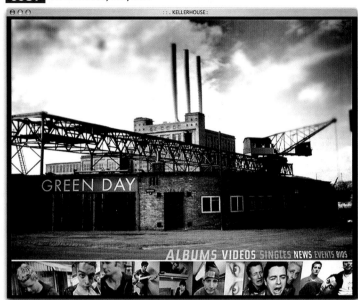

0938 ▶ Fahrenheit Studio, USA

0939 ▶ Edward Mullen Studio, USA

0940 ▶ This Way Design, Norway

0941 ▶ This Way Design, Norway

0942 ▶ Stoltze Design, USA

0943 ▶ Stoltze Design, USA

0944 ▶ Stoltze Design, USA

285

Paraphernalia

0945 Stoltze Design, USA

0946 Stoltze Design, USA

0947 Stoltze Design, USA

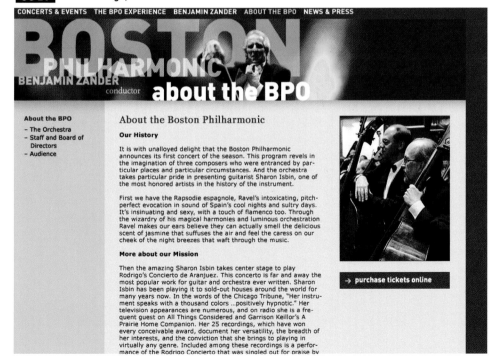

0949 ▶ Gary St. Clare, USA

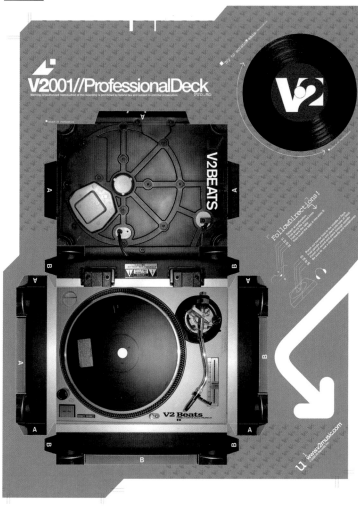

0950 ▶ Gary St. Clare, USA

0952 ▶ Rehab Design, USA

0951 ▶ Sagmeister, Inc., USA

0953 Angela Lorenz, Germany

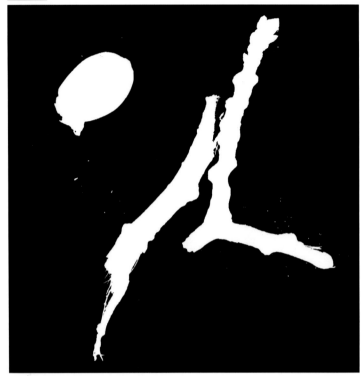

0954 Angela Lorenz, Germany

0955 Angela Lorenz, Germany

0956 Angela Lorenz, Germany

0958 ► Pigeonhole Design, USA

0959 ► Pigeonhole Design, USA

0960 ► Pigeonhole Design, USA

0961 ► Pigeonhole Design, USA

0962 ► Pigeonhole Design, USA

0963 ▶ Detail Design Studio, Ireland

0964 ▶ Detail Design Studio, Ireland

0965 ▶ Segura Inc., USA

0966 ▶ Segura Inc., USA

0967 ▶ **Sebastianruehl.de::Design & Illustration,** Germany

0968 ▶ **Sebastianruehl.de::Design & Illustration,** Germany

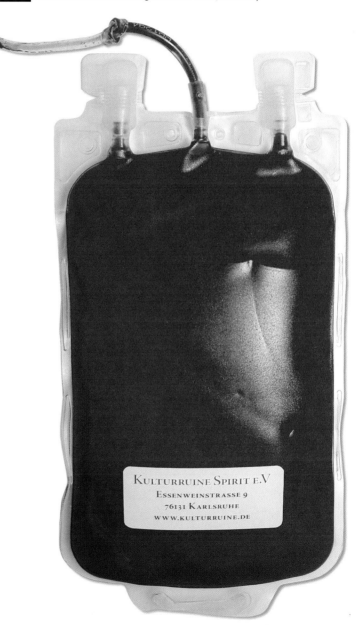

0969 ▶ **Seripop,** Canada

0970 ▶ **Art Chantry Design,** USA

0971 ▶ **Detail Design Studio,** Ireland

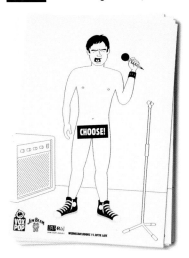

0972 ▶ **Art Chantry Design,** USA

0973 ▶ Licher Art & Design, USA

0974 ▶ Licher Art & Design, USA

0975 ▶ Licher Art & Design, USA

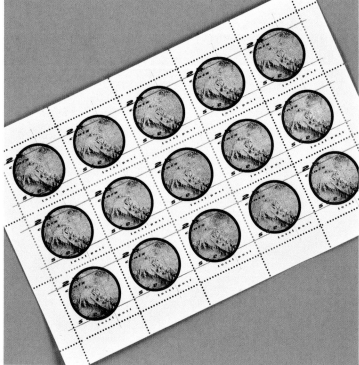

0976 ▶ Licher Art & Design, USA

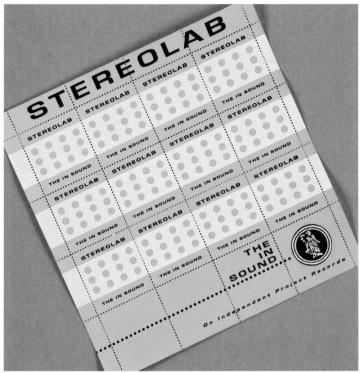

0977 ▶ Licher Art & Design, USA

0978 ▶ Hammerpress, USA

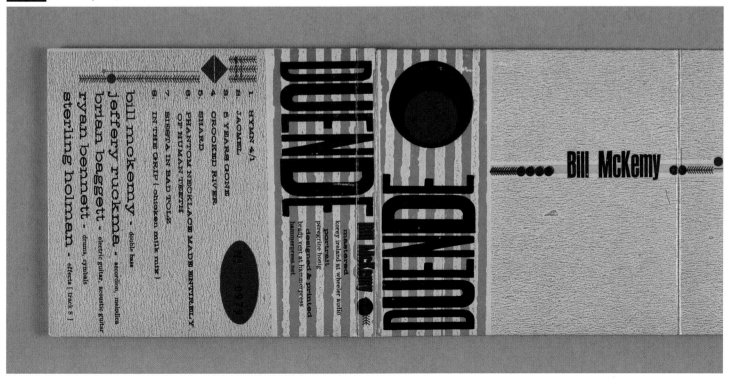

0980 ▶ Funnel : Eric Kass : Utilitarian + Commercial + Fine Art, USA

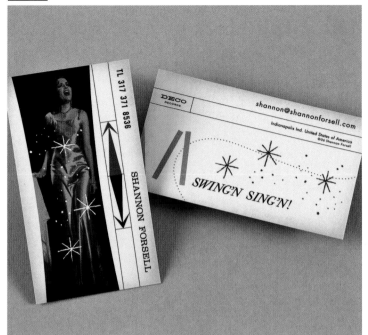

0981 ▶ Benjamin Shaykin, USA

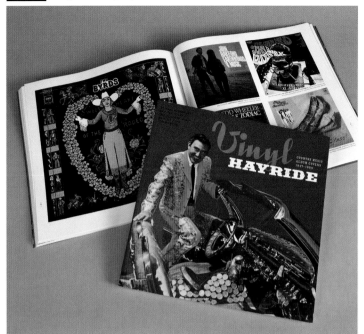

0982 ▶ Tait Hawes, USA

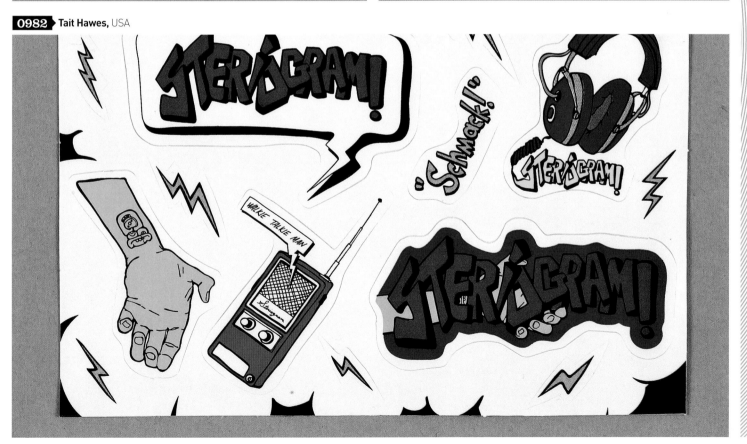

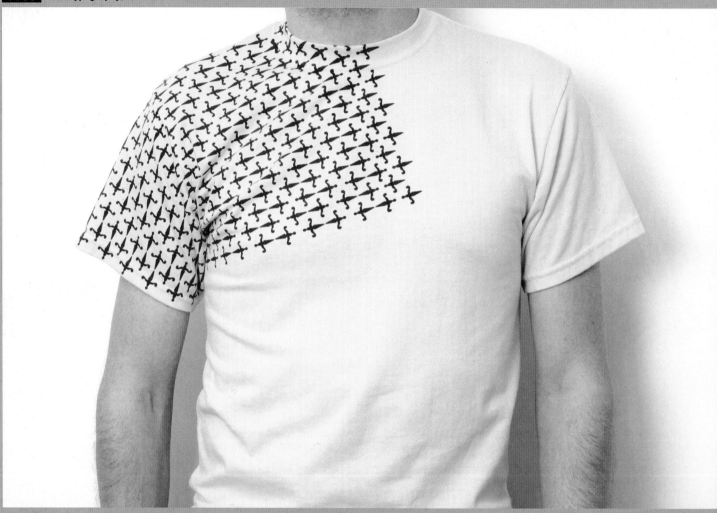

0984 ▶ **Segura Inc.,** USA

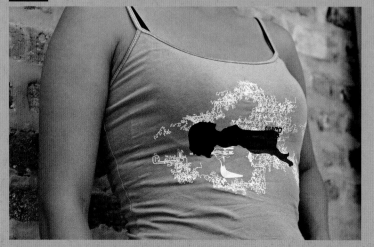

0985 ▶ **Segura Inc.,** USA

0986 ▶ Form, UK

0987 ▶ Form, UK

0988 ▸ **Sagmeister, Inc.,** USA

0989 ▸ **Sibley Peteet Design of Dallas,** USA

0990 ▸ **Post Typography,** USA

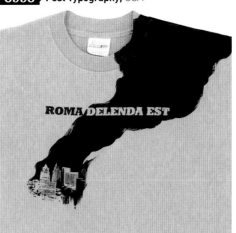

0991 ▸ **Art Guy Studios,** USA

0992 ▸ **Detail Design Studio,** Ireland

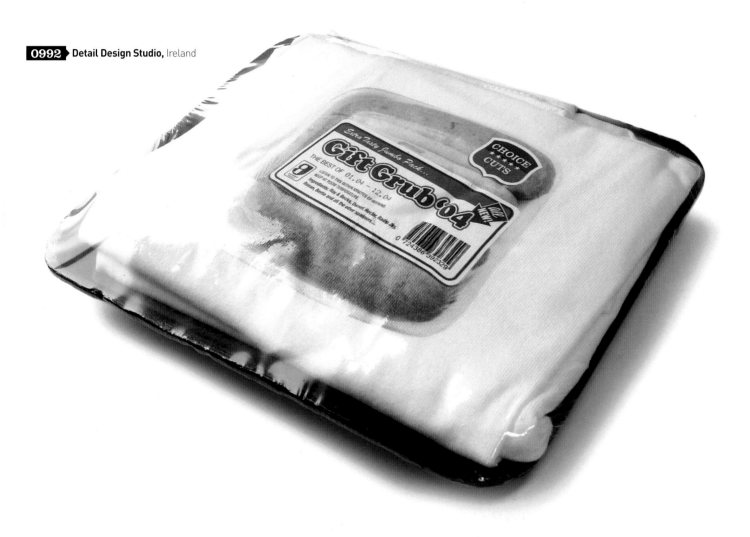

0993 ▸ Art Chantry Design, USA

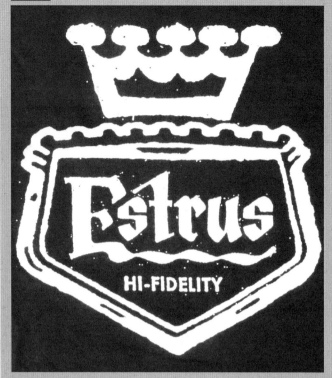

0994 ▸ Art Chantry Design, USA

0995 ▸ Art Chantry Design, USA

0996 ▸ Alphabet Arm Design, USA

0997 ▶ Alphabet Arm Design, USA

0998 ▶ Alphabet Arm Design, USA

1000 ▶ Alphabet Arm Design, USA

0999 ▶ Alphabet Arm Design, USA

Index

by Agency

1 UP

Joakim Jansson
Ovre Gate 5
Oslo/Oslo/0551
Norway
+47 934 55 222
joakim@1-up.com

0215
ART DIRECTOR
Joakim Jansson
DESIGNER
Joakim Jansson
CLIENT
Manual Design

Adam & Co.

Adam Larson
Boston, MA
USA
617-875-2075
adamlarson@gmail.
com

0195, 0433–0435,
0628–0636

Aesthetic Apparatus

Michael Byzewski
27 N. 4th Street, #304
Minneapolis, MN 55401
USA
612-339-3345
Michael@
aestheticapparatus.
com

0144, 0147, 0193,
0341, 0525–0538,
0560, 0685–0688,
0769, 0815

Airside

Anne Brassier
24 Cross St.
London N1 286
UK
+44 20 7354 9912
anne@airside.co.uk

0196
ART DIRECTOR
Fred Deakin
DESIGNER
Fred Deakin
CLIENT
Fred Deakin

Alfalfa

Rafael Esquer
255 Centre St.
7th Floor
New York, NY 10013
USA
212-629-9550
raf@alfalfastudio.com

0224–0226
CREATIVE DIRECTOR
Eiko Ishioka
DESIGNER
Rafael Esquer
CLIENT
Bjork, One Little Indian
Records

Alphabet Arm Design

Aaron Belyea
500 Harrison Ave. 3R
Boston MA 02118
USA
617-451-9990
info@alphabetarm.com

0833
ART DIRECTOR
Aaron Belyea
DESIGNERS
Aaron Belyea, Ryan
Frease
CLIENT
Thought Wizard
Productions

0834
DESIGNER
Aaron Belyea
CLIENT
WKPE

0996
ART DIRECTOR
Aaron Belyea
DESIGNER
Ryan Frease
CLIENT
JDub Records

0997, 1000
ART DIRECTOR
Aaron Belyea
DESIGNER
Ryan Frease
CLIENT
Cinder Block, Inc.

0998, 0999
DESIGNER
Aaron Belyea
CLIENT
Straylight Run, LLC.

Ames Bros

Barry Ament
2118 8th Ave.
Suite 106
Seattle, WA 98121
USA
206-516-3020
barry@amesbros.com

0618, 0620, 0622–
0624, 0626, 0658
DESIGNER
Barry Ament
CLIENT
Pearl Jam

0619, 0621
DESIGNER
Coby Schultz
CLIENT
Pearl Jam

0625
DESIGNER
Coby Schultz
CLIENT
Moe

0627
DESIGNER
Coby Schultz
CLIENT
Superfly

0657
DESIGNER
Coby Schultz
CLIENT
House of Blues

0659, 0661
DESIGNER
Coby Schultz
CLIENT
Neumos

0660
DESIGNER
Coby Schultz

0827
ART DIRECTOR
Jim De Barros
DESIGNER
Coby Schultz
CLIENT
mtvU

0828
DESIGNER
Barry Ament
CLIENT
Mtv

0879, 0880
DESIGNERS
Barry Ament, Coby
Schultz
CLIENT
Ten Club

Andersen M. Studio

10 Aylesbury Suites
City View House
455-463 Bethnal Green
Road
London, E2, 9QY
UK
+44 (0)20 7739 3918

0379–0381
ART DIRECTOR
Martin Andersen
DESIGNER
Martin Andersen
CLIENT
All Saints Records

0382, 0383,
0387, 0388
ART DIRECTOR
Martin Andersen
DESIGNER
Martin Andersen
CLIENT
Enjoy Your Parrot

0384, 0386
ART DIRECTOR
Martin Andersen
DESIGNER
Martin Andersen
CLIENT
Piano Magic

0385
ART DIRECTOR
Martin Andersen
DESIGNER
Martin Andersen
CLIENT
4AD Records

Angela Lorenz

c/o Buro fur Film und
Gestaltung
10119 Berlin
Germany
0049 (0)177 2581687
info@alorenz.net

0092
DESIGNERS
Angela Lorenz
CLIENT
Mitek, Berlin/
Stockholm

0093
DESIGNER
Angela Lorenz
CLIENT
Data Error, Berlin

0094–0097
DESIGNER
Angela Lorenz
CLIENT
Silke Maurer, Berlin

0098–0106
DESIGNERS
Lorenz and Berlin
CLIENT
Orthlorng Musark

0476–0479, 0481,
0483
DESIGNER
Angela Lorenz
CLIENT
Kitty – Yo, Berlin

0480
DESIGNERS
Angela Lorenz,
Stephen Mathieu
CLIENT
Staalplaat

0482
DESIGNER
Angela Lorenz
CLIENT
Tigerbeat 6

0953–0956
DESIGNER
Angela Lorenz
CLIENT
Mitek

Art Chantry Design

Art Chantry
P.O. Box 9216
Tacoma, WA 98490
USA
253-310-3993
art@artchantry.com

0007–0017, 0545–
0548, 0970, 0972,
0993–0995
ART DIRECTOR
Art Chantry
DESIGNER
Art Chantry

Art Guy Studios

James F. Kraus
195 W. Canton St.
Boston, MA 02116
USA
617-437-1945
jck@artguy.com

0843
ART DIRECTOR
James F. Kraus
DESIGNER
James F. Kraus
CLIENT
Chez Moi Records

Chunklet Graphic Control

Henry Howings
P.O. Box 2814
Athens, GA 30612
USA
404-423-6547
henry@chunklet.com

0779
ART DIRECTOR
Henry Howings
CLIENT
The Earl

0780
ART DIRECTOR
Henry Howings
CLIENT
Chunklet Magazine

Dan Stiles

2928 NE 11th
Portland, OR 07212
USA
503-806-4670
dan@danstiles.com

0568–0571, 0573,
0574, 0576, 0577
ART DIRECTOR
Dan Stiles
DESIGNER
Dan Stiles
CLIENT
Mon Qui Presents

0572
ART DIRECTOR
Dan Stiles
DESIGNER
Dan Stiles
CLIENT
The Doug Fir Lounge

Design by Frank Scheikl

Tina Frank
Mayerhofgasse 20/6
1040 Vienna
Austria
+43 1 505 60 66
welcome@
frankscheikl.com

0497, 0498
ART DIRECTOR
Tina Frank
DESIGNER
Tina Frank
CLIENT
Mego

desres design group

Michaela Kessler
Kaiserstrasse 69
Frankfurt/
Hessen/60329
Germany
++49 (0)69 458220
contact@desres.de

0120–0122
ART DIRECTORS
Dirk Schrod,
Michaela Kessler
DESIGNERS
Michaela Kessler,
Dirk Schrod
CLIENT
pooledmusic

0450
ART DIRECTOR
Dirk Schrod
DESIGNER
Dirk Schrod
CLIENT
neuton

Detail Design Studio

11 The Friary, Bow St.
Smithfield, Dublin
Ireland
+353.1.8783168
mail@detail.ie

0963–0964
ART DIRECTOR
Detail Design Studio
DESIGNER
Detail Design Studio
CLIENT
Detail Design Studio

0971
ART DIRECTOR
Detail Design Studio
DESIGNER
Detail Design Studio
CLIENT
Rock'n'Roll Rescue
Squad

0992
ART DIRECTOR
Detail Design Studio
DESIGNER
Detail Design Studio
CLIENT
EMI Music Ireland

Diana Sudyka

2020 Darrow Ave.
Evanston, IL 60201
USA
773-425-7845
Diana@dianasudyka.com

0801, 0804
DESIGNER
Diana Sudyka
CLIENT
The Decemberists

0803
DESIGNER
Diana Sudyka
CLIENT
The Zincs/Edith Frost

DJG Design

Danny J. Gibson
1118 West 40th St.
Kansas City, MO 64111
USA
816-531-0651
djgdesign@hotmail.
com

0451, 0777
ART DIRECTOR
Danny J. Gibson
DESIGNER
Danny J. Gibson
CLIENT
Dan Talmadge

0776
ART DIRECTOR
Danny J. Gibson
DESIGNER
Danny J. Gibson
CLIENT
Eldir

0778
ART DIRECTOR
Danny J. Gibson
DESIGNER
Danny J. Gibson
CLIENT
Darling At Sea

0781
ART DIRECTOR
Danny J. Gibson
DESIGNER
Danny J. Gibson
CLIENT
Elevator Division

Douze Studio

Lars P. Kromse
Schanzenstr. 25
01037 Dresden
Germany
0175/2429490
larspkromse@gmx.de

0594, 0816–0817
DESIGNER
Lars P Kromze
CLIENT
Booker

Earwig Studio

Martin Sorger
34 High Street
Ipswich, MA 01938
USA
978-473-0057
m.sorger@hotmail.com

0452
ART DIRECTOR
Martin Sorger
CLIENT
Projekt

Edward Mullen Studio

Edward Mullen
63 Sherman Pl., E3
Jersey City, NJ 07307
USA
718-809-9079
ed@edmullen.com

0913–0916
ART DIRECTOR
Edward Mullen
DESIGNER
Edward Mullen
CLIENT
Brendan Benson/V2
Records

0917–0920
ART DIRECTOR
Edward Mullen
DESIGNER
Edward Mullen
CLIENT
Blanche

0921
ART DIRECTOR
Edward Mullen
DESIGNER
Edward Mullen
CLIENT
Gosling/V2 Records

0939
ART DIRECTOR
Edward Mullen
DESIGNER
Edward Mullen
CLIENT
The Citizens Band/
Press Here

EPOS, Inc.

Mariko Ostboe
1639 16th St.
Santa Monica, CA
90404
USA
310-581-2418
mariko@eposinc.com

0397
ART DIRECTOR
Gabrielle Raumberger
DESIGNER
Eric Martinez
CLIENT
Spiral Subwave
Records International

Fahrenheit Studio

Dylan Tran
10303 Mississippi Ave.
Los Angeles, CA 90025
USA
310-282-8422
info@fahrenheit.com

0938
ART DIRECTORS
Dylan Tran,
Robert Weitz
DESIGNERS
Dylan Tran,
Robert Weitz
CLIENT
Virgin Records America

FarmBarn Art Co.

Drue Dixon
150 East Main St.
Unit 212
Columbus, OH 43215
USA

0582–0587,
0589–0593,
0596–0597
ART DIRECTORS
Drue Dixon,
Mike Pierce
CLIENT
PromoWest
Productions

0588
ART DIRECTORS
Drue Dixon,
Mike Pierce
CLIENT
The Hush Sound

Fluid

Mark Harris
12 Tenby St.
Birmingham, B1 3AJ
UK
+44 (0) 121 212 0121
mark@fluiddesign.co.uk

0391
ART DIRECTOR
Gary St. Clare
DESIGNER
Gary St. Clare
CLIENT
Verve Jazz

0427
ART DIRECTOR
Gary St. Clare
DESIGNER
Gary St. Clare
CLIENT
V2 Records

0846, 0847, 0850, 0852
ART DIRECTOR
Gary St. Clare
DESIGNER
Gary St. Clare
CLIENT
V2 Records/Sunshine Enterprises

0949, 0950
ART DIRECTOR
Gary St. Clare
DESIGNER
Gary St. Clare
CLIENT
V2 Records

GDC

Chris Dixon
33 Baxter St.
Fortitude Valley
QLD, 4006
Australia
+61 7 3252 1500
chris@gdesign.com.au

0444, 0446
ART DIRECTOR
Stewart De Lacey
DESIGNER
Chris Dixon
CLIENT
MRA Entertainment

0445
ART DIRECTOR
Chris Dixon
DESIGNER
Chris Dixon
CLIENT
Women in Docs

Ghost Ranch Studio

Yasutaka Kato
5-17-5 Yutaka-cha
Shinagawa-ku
Tokyo 142-0042
Japan
03-3788-4563
ghostranch-kato@
crest.ocu.ne.jp

0182–0185
ART DIRECTOR
Yasutaka Kato
DESIGNER
Yasutaka Kato
CLIENT
Kiloon Sony Records

0602
CLIENT
Sui Sei

0603, 0604
ART DIRECTOR
Yasutaka Kato
DESIGNER
Yasutaka Kato
CLIENT
SONY Records

Go Welsh

Craig Welsh
987 Mill Mar Rd.
Lancaster, PA 17601
USA
717-898-9000
cwelsh@gowelsh.com

0872–0874
CLIENT
Music For Everyone

Grady & Metcalf

Colin Metcalf
1334 W. Wolfram St.
Chicago, IL 60657
USA
773-296-9400
colin@gumworld.com

0854–0871
ART DIRECTORS
Kevin Grady, Colin Metcalf
DESIGNERS
Kevin Grady, Colin Metcalf

Grandpeople

Magnus Helgesen
Mollendalsveien 17
5009 Bergen
Norway
+47 45 26 02 27
post@grandpeople.org

0264, 0265
DESIGNER
Grandpeople
CLIENT
Enlightenment

0342–0345
DESIGNER
Grandpeople
CLIENT
Kompakt/Digitalo Enterprises

0346–0348
DESIGNER
Grandpeople
CLIENT
Digitalo Enterprises

0349, 0350
DESIGNER
Grandpeople
CLIENT
Melektronikk

0351, 0352
DESIGNER
Grandpeople
CLIENT
Simax

0353
DESIGNER
Grandpeople
CLIENT
Enlightenment

0354, 0355
DESIGNER
Grandpeople
CLIENT
Creaked Records

0605
DESIGNER
Grandpeople
CLIENT
Melektronikk

0826
DESIGNER
Grandpeople
CLIENT
Creaked Records

Gravillis, Inc.

Kenny Gravillis
1266 Meadowbrook Ave.
Los Angeles, CA 90019
USA
323-935-9347
studio@gravillisinc.com

0295–0298
ART DIRECTOR
Kenny Gravillis
DESIGNERS
Kenny Gravillis,
Russell Robinson 2
CLIENT
MCA Records

0299, 0300
ART DIRECTOR
Kenny Gravillis
DESIGNER
Gravillis Inc.
CLIENT
Concord Records

0429
ART DIRECTOR
Kenny Gravillis
DESIGNER
Gravillis Inc.
CLIENT
Motown Records

0514
ART DIRECTOR
Kenny Gravillis
DESIGNERS
Kenny Gravillis,
Russell Robinson 2
CLIENT
MCA Records

Hammerpress

Brady Vest
1919 Wyandotte, Studio B
Kansas City, MO 64108
USA
816-421-1929
sales@hammerpress.net

0524
ART DIRECTOR
Brady Vest
DESIGNER
Brady Vest
CLIENT
TJ Dovebelly

0578–0581
ART DIRECTOR
Brady Vest
DESIGNER
Brady Vest
CLIENT
eleven productions

0795
ART DIRECTOR
Brady Vest
DESIGNER
Matt McNary

0978
ART DIRECTOR
Brady Vest
DESIGNER
Brady Vest
CLIENT
Bill McKemy

Hatch Show Print

Brad Vetter
316 Broadway
Nashville, TN 37201
USA
615-256-2805
hatchshowprint@
bellsouth.net

0606
ART DIRECTOR
Brad Vetter
DESIGNER
Brad Vetter
CLIENT
Live Nation

0607
ART DIRECTOR
Agnes Barton-Sabo
DESIGNER
Agnes Barton-Sabo
CLIENT
Live Nation

0608
ART DIRECTOR
Agnes Barton-Sabo
DESIGNER
Agnes Barton-Sabo
CLIENT
Ryman Auditorium

0609–0611
ART DIRECTOR
Julie Sola
DESIGNER
Julie Sola
CLIENT
Live Nation

0612
ART DIRECTOR
Brad Vetter
DESIGNER
Brad Vetter
CLIENT
Ballroom Marfa

0613
ART DIRECTOR
Nieves Uhl
DESIGNER
Nieves Uhl
CLIENT
The Royal Deuces

0614
ART DIRECTOR
Nieves Uhl
DESIGNER
Nieves Uhl
CLIENT
Bill Wence Promotions

0615
ART DIRECTOR
Jim Sherraden
DESIGNER
Jim Sherraden

House of Graphics

Gina Lucia
212 Columbus Ave.
Palisades Park, NJ
07650
USA
201-321-5945
gina@houseofgrfx.com

0448
ART DIRECTOR
Gina Lucia
DESIGNER
Gina Lucia
CLIENT
Plastic Passion

JSDS

Justin Skeesuck
7630 Marie Ave.
La Mesa, CA 91941
USA
619-277-2585
hello@jsds.us

0192
ART DIRECTOR
JSDS
DESIGNER
Justin Skeesuck
CLIENT
Ryan Calhoun

Judson Design

Jeff Davis
2407 Norfolk St.
Houston, TX 77098
USA
512-557-4128
jeff@judsondesign.com

0832
ART DIRECTOR
Jeff Davis
DESIGNER
Jeff Davis
CLIENT
Theo Entertainment
Group

Jutoju

Toby Cornish
Brunnenstr. 191
Berlin 10119
Germany
+49 30-28093946
info@jutojo.de

0216–0219
ART DIRECTOR
Jutojo
DESIGNER
Jutojo
CLIENT
JCR Records, Munich

Karim Rashid, Inc.

Molly Nadler
357 W. 17th St.
New York, NY 10011
USA
212-929-8657
office@karimrashid.com

0197
DESIGNER
Karim Rashid
CLIENT
Obliqsound

karlssonwilker inc.

536 6th Ave.
2nd Floor
New York, NY 10011
212-929-8063

0205–0214,
0255–0260, 0322,
0735–0737

Kellerhouse, Inc.

Neil Kellerhouse
3781 Greenwood Ave.
Mar Vista, CA 90066
USA
310-776-1234
neil@kellerhouse.com

0275, 0276
ART DIRECTOR
Neil Kellerhouse
DESIGNER
Neil Kellerhouse
CLIENT
Triple X Records

0280–0283
ART DIRECTOR
Neil Kellerhouse
DESIGNER
Neil Kellerhouse
CLIENT
Rhino Records

0284–0289
ART DIRECTOR
Neil Kellerhouse
DESIGNERS
Neil Kellerhouse,
Peter Grant
CLIENT
Rhino Records

0408–0410
ART DIRECTORS
Neil Kellerhouse,
Hugh Brown
DESIGNER
Neil Kellerhouse
CLIENT
Rhino Records

0431
ART DIRECTOR
Neil Kellerhouse
DESIGNER
Neil Kellerhouse
CLIENT
A + M Records

0936, 0937
ART DIRECTOR
Neil Kellerhouse
DESIGNER
Neil Kellerhouse
CLIENT
Warner Bros.

Kiki Ikura

101 Monmouth St.
#510
Brookline, MA 02446
USA
857-272-0652
babedeboo@gmail.com

0340
DESIGNER
Kiki Ikura
CLIENT
Flavour of Sound

Kinetic Singapore

Pann Lim
2 Leng Kee Rd.
#03-02, Thye Hong
Centre
S 159086
Singapore
+65 6479 6802

0301–0303
ART DIRECTORS
Leng Soh, Pann Lim,
Roy Poh
DESIGNERS
Leng Soh, Pann Lim,
Roy Poh
CLIENT
Concave Scream

Kim Hiorthøy

Lives and works in Oslo
and Berlin

0199

Kymtra Design

Ralph Centra
18 Diamond St., 2L
Brooklyn, NY 11222
USA
917-804-6640
Ralph@kymtradesign.com

0198
ART DIRECTOR
Ralph Centra
DESIGNER
Ralph Cantra
CLIENT
Embryo Music

LeBoYe

Ignatius Hermawan
Tanzil
J1 Kemang Selatan
No. 99 A
Jakarta Selatan 12730
Indonesia
+6221 7199676
tanzil@leboyedesign.com

0202
ART DIRECTOR
Ignatius Hermawan
Tanzil
DESIGNERS
Ignatius Hermawan
Tanzil, Grace Patricia
CLIENT
LeBoYe

LeDouxville

Jesse LeDoux
21 Sixth St.
Providence, RI 02906
USA
401-437-6090
info@ledouxville.com

0050–0052,
0201, 0561
ART DIRECTOR
Jesse LeDoux
DESIGNER
Jesse LeDoux
CLIENT
Sub Pop Records

0053, 0054, 0565
ART DIRECTOR
Jesse LeDoux
DESIGNER
Jesse LeDoux
CLIENT
Suicide Squeeze
Records

0055, 0056
ART DIRECTOR
Jesse LeDoux
DESIGNER
Jesse LeDoux
CLIENT
Speaker Speaker

0562
ART DIRECTOR
Jesse LeDoux
DESIGNER
Jesse LeDoux
CLIENT
Jetstream

0563
ART DIRECTOR
Jesse LeDoux
DESIGNER
Jesse LeDoux
CLIENT
The Little Ones

0564
ART DIRECTOR
Jesse LeDoux
DESIGNER
Jesse LeDoux
CLIENT
House of Blues

0566, 0567
ART DIRECTOR
Jesse LeDoux
DESIGNER
Jesse LeDoux
CLIENT
The Showbox

Licher Art & Design

Bruce Licher
45 Castle Rock Rd., #3
Sedona, AZ 86351
USA
928-284-1282
land@esedona.not

0441–0443
ART DIRECTOR
Bruce Licher
DESIGNER
Bruce Licher
CLIENT
Independent Project
Records

0442
ART DIRECTOR
Bruce Licher
DESIGNER
Bruce Licher
CLIENT
St. Ives Records

0443
ART DIRECTOR
Bruce Licher
DESIGNER
Bruce Licher
CLIENT
Licher Art & Design

0523
ART DIRECTOR
Bruce Licher
DESIGNER
Bruce Licher
CLIENT
Hidden Agenda
Records

Osso Design

Julaio Villas
Rua Sao Domingos do
Prata, 735
Santo Antonio
Belo Horizonte – MG
– 30330-110
Brazil
+55(31)3296.0696
juliao@osso.com.br

0932, 0933
ART DIRECTOR
Fred Paulino
DESIGNER
Fred Paulino
CLIENT
Mercado Moderno

Patent Pending

Jeff Kleinsmith
6708 9th Ave., NW
Seattle, WA 98117
USA
206-428-1333
jeff@patentpending
industries.com

0549
ART DIRECTOR
Jeff Kleinsmith
DESIGNER
Jeff Kleinsmith
CLIENT
The Moore Theatre

0550, 0552, 0554,
0556, 0558
ART DIRECTOR
Jeff Kleinsmith
DESIGNER
Jeff Kleinsmith
CLIENT
The Showbox

0551
ART DIRECTOR
Jeff Kleinsmith
DESIGNER
Jeff Kleinsmith
CLIENT
Neumo's

0553
ART DIRECTOR
Jeff Kleinsmith
DESIGNER
Jeff Kleinsmith
CLIENT
Kinski

0555
ART DIRECTOR
Jeff Kleinsmith
DESIGNER
Jeff Kleinsmith
CLIENT
Paramount Theatre

0557
ART DIRECTORS
Jeff Kleinsmith
DESIGNER
Jeff Kleinsmith
CLIENT
Wilco

0559
ART DIRECTOR
Jeff Kleinsmith
DESIGNER
Jeff Kleinsmith
CLIENT
House of Blues

Pigeonhole Design

Brad Rhodes
136 Stillman St. #3
San Francisco, CA
94107
USA
415-592-3331
brad@eudesco.com

0958–0962
ART DIRECTOR
Todd Baldwin
DESIGNER
Todd Baldwin
CLIENT
human machine

Plazm Media

Sarah Gottesdiener
P.O. Box 2863
PDX, OR 97208
USA
502-528-8000
sarahg@plazm.com

0318–0320,
0323–0325,
0774, 0838

Post Typography

Bruce Willen
3220 Guilford Ave.
Suite 3
Baltimore, MD 21218
410-889-7469
info@posttypography.
com

0438, 0440
ART DIRECTORS
Bruce Willen, Nolen
Strals
DESIGNERS
Bruce Willen, Nolen
Strals
CLIENTS
Double Dagger

0706
ART DIRECTORS
Bruce Willen, Nolen
Strals
DESIGNERS
Bruce Willen, Nolen
Strals
CLIENT
Double Dagger

0707, 0830
ART DIRECTOR
Bruce Willen
DESIGNER
Bruce Willen
CLIENT
The Ottobar

0708
ART DIRECTORS
Bruce Willen, Nolen
Strals
DESIGNERS
Bruce Willen, Nolen
Strals
CLIENT
Millersville University
AIGA

0709
ART DIRECTORS
Bruce Willen, Nolen
Strals
DESIGNERS
Bruce Willen, Nolen
Strals
CLIENT
Wham City

0710, 0711
ART DIRECTOR
Nolen Strals
DESIGNER
Nolen Strals
CLIENT
The Ottobar

0787
ART DIRECTORS
Bruce Willen, Nolen
Strals
DESIGNERS
Bruce Willen, Nolen
Strals
CLIENT
Atom And His Package

0983
ART DIRECTORS
Bruce Willen, Nolen
Strals
DESIGNER
Bruce Willen
CLIENT
Double Dagger

0990
ART DIRECTOR
Nolen Strals
DESIGNER
Nolen Strals
CLIENT
Roma Delenda Est
Power of Beauty Co.,
Ltd.

Power of Beauty Co., Ltd.

Mic*Itaya
4-41-18 Kamimeguro
Meguro-Ku
Tokyo 153-0051
Japan
813-3712-8521
pobdesign@micitaya.
com

0200, 0203
ART DIRECTOR
Mic*Itaya
DESIGNER
Noriyuki Yokota
CLIENTS
Bridge Inc.

0227
ART DIRECTOR
Mic*Itaya
DESIGNER
Noriyuki Yokota
CLIENT
Polystar Co., LTD

0228
ART DIRECTOR
Mic*Itaya
DESIGNER
Noriyuki Yokota
CLIENT
Earthly Nine Inc.

0510
ART DIRECTOR
Mic*Itaya
DESIGNER
Noriyuki Yokota
CLIENT
Bridge Inc.

Powerslide Design Co.

Mike Klay
1415 6th Ave. N. #405
Seattle, WA 98109
USA
206-853-2633
mike@
powerslidedesign.com

0799
DESIGNER
Mike Klay
CLIENT
Neumo's

0800
DESIGNER
Mike Klay
CLIENT
Death Cab For Cutie

Red Design

Keith Davey
Studio 1, 11 Jew St.
Brighton
BN 2NL
UK
01273 704614
info@red-design.co.uk

0220–0223
ART DIRECTOR
Red Design
DESIGNER
Red Design
CLIENTS
Station 55

0495, 0496
ART DIRECTOR
Red Design
DESIGNER
Red Design
CLIENT
Rise Robots Rise

Rehab Design

Gary St. Clare
319 E. 25th St., #1B
New York City, NY
10010
USA
917-517-2803
saintclare@hotmail

0087–0091, 0948
ART DIRECTOR
Gary St. Clare/ David
Culderley
DESIGNER
Gary St. Clare
CLIENT
V2 Records

0952
ART DIRECTOR
Gary St. Clare
DESIGNER
Gary St. Clare
CLIENT
V2 Decals

re-public

Morten Windelev
Laplandsgade 4
DK-2300 Copenhagen
Denmark
+45 7020 9890
windelev@re-public.
com

0305
ART DIRECTOR
Romeo Vidner
DESIGNER
Romeo Vidner
CLIENT
Copenhagen Jazz
Festival

Richard May

404 Clerkenwell
Workshops
London EC1R OAT
UK
+44 (0)207014 3830
rich@richard-may.com

0145
ART DIRECTOR
Richard May
DESIGNER
Richard May
CLIENT
Punish the Atom/ 48
Crash

Rick Myers

P.O. Box 225
Manchester M22 4UH
UK
rickmyers@
footprintsinthesnow.
co.uk

0307–0311
ART DIRECTOR
Rick Myers
DESIGNER
Rick Myers
CLIENT
Rebelski

0308, 0310
ART DIRECTOR
Rick Myers
DESIGNER
Rick Myers
CLIENT
John Cale/EMI

0309
ART DIRECTOR
Rick Myers
DESIGNER
Rick Myers
CLIENT
Dinosaur Jr.

0311
ART DIRECTOR
Rick Myers
DESIGNER
Rick Myers
CLIENT
Doves/EMI

0751
ART DIRECTOR
Rick Myers
DESIGNER
Rick Myers
CLIENT
Flywheel,
Easthampton, MA

0752
ART DIRECTOR
Rick Myers
DESIGNER
Rick Myers
CLIENT
Doves/EMI

Rinzen

Adrian Clifford
P.O. Box 1729
New Farm
Brisbane QLD 4005
Australia
+617 3358 3418
adrain@rinzen.com

0161, 0162
ART DIRECTOR
Rinzen
DESIGNER
Craig Redman
CLIENT
Below Par Records

0163
ART DIRECTOR
Rinzen
DESIGNER
Karl Maier
CLIENT
Pop Frenzy Records

0164
ART DIRECTOR
Rinzen
DESIGNER
Craig Redman
CLIENT
Egg Records

**Robert
Beerman**

16 Newman St.
Cambridge, MA 02140
USA
617-864-7754
beermanleshock@
comcast.net

0519
DESIGNER
Robert Beerman
CLIENT
Cut-Out/Starlight
Furniture Company

**Rune
Mortensen
Design Studio**

Rune Mortensen
Brenneriveien 9
0182 Oslo
Norway
+47 22 1 04 50
post@runemortensen.no

0165–0167,
0356–0359
ART DIRECTOR
Rune Mortensen
DESIGNER
Rune Mortensen
CLIENTS
Smalltown Super Jazz
Pro Musica
Grappa
CCAP

Sagmeister, Inc.

Stefan Sagmeister
222 W. 14th St.
New York, NY 10011
USA
212-647-1789
Stefan@sagmeister.com

0360–0378, 0754,
0897–0901, 0951,
0988

**Sayles Graphic
Design**

Sheree Clark
3701 Beaver Ave.
Des Moines, IA 50310
USA
515-279-2922
sheree@saylesdesign.
com

0831
ART DIRECTOR
John Sayles
DESIGNER
John Sayles
CLIENT
Sexicide

Scott King

33 Kelvin Road
London N5 2PR
UK
+44 207 359 2316
info@scottking.co.uk

0128–0129

**Seattle Show
Posters**

Rick Goral
P.O. Box 61123
Seattle, WA 98141
USA
206-972-3189
rick@speakeasy.net

0641
ART DIRECTOR
Rick Goral
DESIGNER
Rick Goral

**Sebastian-
ruehl.de::
Design &
Illustration**

Sebastian Buhl
Kreuzstrasse 36
44139 Dortmund
Germany
+49 231-137 04 70
info@sebastianruehl.de

0967, 0968
ART DIRECTOR
Sebastian Ruhl
DESIGNER
Sebastian Ruhl
CLIENT
Kulturruine Spirit E.V.

Segura, Inc.

Carlos Segura
1110 North Milwaukee
Ave.
Chicago, IL 60622-4017
USA
773-862-1214
carlos@segura-inc.com

0190, 0464, 0465,
0730, 0965, 0966,
0984, 0985
ART DIRECTOR
Carlos Segura
DESIGNER
Carlos Segura
CLIENT
NYCO

Seripop

Yannick Desranleau
P.O. Box 226,
Station "B"
Montreal, QC
H3B3J7
Canada
514-768-1320
info@seripop.com

0416
ART DIRECTORS
Yannick Desranleau,
Chloe Lum
DESIGNERS
Yannick Desranleau,
Chloe Lum
CLIENT
Merge Records

0417
ART DIRECTORS
Yannick Desranleau,
Chloe Lum
DESIGNERS
Yannick Desranleau,
Chloe Lum
CLIENT
Epitaph Records

0418
ART DIRECTORS
Yannick Desranleau,
Chloe Lum
DESIGNERS
Yannick Desranleau,
Chloe Lum
CLIENT
Alien 8 Recordings

0419, 0420
ART DIRECTORS
Yannick Desranleau,
Chloe Lum
DESIGNERS
Yannick Desranleau,
Chloe Lum
CLIENT
Last Gang Records/
DKD/Universal

0724, 0969
ART DIRECTORS
Yannick Desranleau,
Chloe Lum
DESIGNERS
Yannick Desranleau,
Chloe Lum
CLIENT
AIDS Wolf

0725
ART DIRECTORS
Yannick Desranleau,
Chloe Lum
DESIGNERS
Yannick Desranleau,
Chloe Lum
CLIENT
Shawn Scallen

0726
ART DIRECTORS
Yannick Desranleau,
Chloe Lum
DESIGNERS
Yannick Desranleau,
Chloe Lum
CLIENT
Walter's on Washington

0727
ART DIRECTORS
Yannick Desranleau,
Chloe Lum
DESIGNERS
Yannick Desranleau,
Chloe Lum
CLIENT
Justin Gobeil

0728–0729
ART DIRECTORS
Yannick Desranleau,
Chloe Lum
DESIGNERS
Yannick Desranleau,
Chloe Lum
CLIENT
Mandatory Moustache

shed

Russell Mills
Still Point
Millans Park
Ambleside
Cumbria LA22 9AG
UK
44 (0) 1 5394 31278
mills@matter-shed.
co.uk

0326–0335
ART DIRECTOR
Russell Mills
DESIGNERS
Russell Mills, Michael
Webster

Sibley Peteet Design of Dallas

Denise Guerra
3232 McKinney Ave.,
Suite 1200
Dallas, TX 75204
USA
214-969-1050
denise@spddallas.com

0989
DESIGNER
Brandon Kirk
CLIENT
Hendrick

Sidekick

Karen Koch/Chris
Pachunka
1524 Cuning St., Apt 424
Omaha, NE 68102
USA
402-650-8999
Karen@
sidekickdesign.com

0775, 0798,
0805–0811
ART DIRECTOR
Karen Koch/Chris
Pachunka
DESIGNER
Karen Koch/Chris
Pachunka
CLIENT
one percent
productions

Single Son Studios

Tad Carpenter
522 Grand, #4E
Kansas City, MO 64106
USA
913-302-1019
tad@tadcarpenter.com

0790
ART DIRECTOR
Tad Carpenter
DESIGNERS
Tad Carpenter, Dan
Padavic
CLIENT
Eleven Productions

0791
ART DIRECTOR
Tad Carpenter
DESIGNER
Tad Carpenter
CLIENT
Hunt Industries

Skouras Design Inc.

Angela Skouras
56 Studio Hill Rd.
Kent, CT 06757
USA
212-349-0101
angela@skourasdesign.
com

0394–0396
ART DIRECTORS
Angela Skouras,
Howard Fritzson
DESIGNERS
Angela Skouras, Mike
Curry
CLIENT
SONY Music

SMAY Vision

Stan Stanski, Phil
Yarnall
40 W. Main St., #1B
Mount Kisco, NY 10549
USA
914-241-6340
smay@smayvision.com

0403
ART DIRECTORS
Stan Stanski, Phil
Yarnall
DESIGNERS
Stan Stanski, Phil
Yarnall
CLIENT
Time Life

0484
ART DIRECTORS
Stan Stanski, Phil
Yarnall
DESIGNERS
Stan Stanski, Phil
Yarnall
CLIENT
Polydor Records

Soap Design Co.

Gabriela Lopez
2874 Rowena Ave.
Los Angeles, CA 90039
USA
323-666-2383
gaby@soapdesign.com

0454, 0455
ART DIRECTOR
Soap Design Co.
DESIGNER
Soap Design Co.
CLIENT
Transparent Music

SONY BMG

Howard Fritzson
550 Madison Ave.,
#2954
New York, NY 10022
USA
212-833-8223
howardfritzson@
sonybmg.com

0515
ART DIRECTORS
Dan Ichimoto, Howard
Fritzson, Seth
Rothstein
DESIGNER
Dan Ichimoto
CLIENT
Columbia Legacy

Sound in Motion

Pascal Cools
Verdussenstraat 44
2018 Antwerp
Belgium
00 32 3 238 82 17
pascalcools@skynet.be

0662–0665
DESIGNER
Pascal Cools
CLIENT
Kunstencentrum
Belgie

Spotco

Gail Anderson
512 Seventh Ave.,
2nd Floor
New York, NY 10018
USA
646-277-7721
ganderson@spotnyc.
com

0732
ART DIRECTOR
Gail Anderson
DESIGNER
Bashian Aquart
CLIENT
Manhattan Theatre
Club

0733
ART DIRECTOR
Gail Anderson
DESIGNER
Darren Cox
CLIENT
The Producing Office

0734
ART DIRECTOR
Gail Anderson
DESIGNER
Darren Cox, Frank
Gargiulo
CLIENT
James L. Nederlander,
Jr.

0903–0906
ART DIRECTOR
Gail Anderson
DESIGNERS
Jessica Disbrow, Sam
Eckersley, Bashan
Aquart
CLIENT
Random House, Rolling
Stone

Square Zero

Jose Nieto
120 Washington St.,
Suite 202F
Salem, MA 01970
USA
617-953-4589
jose@squarezerostudio.
com

0511
ART DIRECTORS
Jose Nieto, Naomi
Yang
DESIGNER
Jose Nieto
CLIENT
ICA/Boston + Exact
Change

SRG Design

2817 West Silver Lake Dr.
Los Angeles, CA 90030
USA
323-913-9488

0148, 0149
ART DIRECTORS
Susan Lavoie, Steven
R. Gilmore
DESIGNER
Steven R. Gilmore
CLIENT
Virgin Records

0316, 0317
ART DIRECTOR
Steven R. Gilmore
DESIGNER
Steven R. Gilmore
CLIENT
Spitfire Records

0598
ART DIRECTOR
Steven R. Gilmore
DESIGNER
Steven R. Gilmore
CLIENT
Spitfire Records

0599
ART DIRECTORS
Susan Lavoie for
Den45@EMI, Steven R.
Gilmore
DESIGNER
Steven R. Gilmore
CLIENT
Virgin Records

0600
ART DIRECTOR
Steven R. Gilmore
DESIGNER
Steven R. Gilmore
CLIENT
The Tiger Lillies

Stefan Kassel Design

Stefan Kassel
Gartnerstrasse 99
20253 Hamburg
Germany
stefankassel@
stefankassel.com

0057–0077
DESIGNER
Stefan Kassel

The Small Stakes

Jason Munn
1847 5th Ave.
Oakland, CA 94606
USA
510-507-9466
jason@thesmallstakes.com

0644
ART DIRECTOR
Jason Munn
DESIGNER
Jason Munn
CLIENT
Rogue Wave

0645
ART DIRECTOR
Jason Munn
DESIGNER
Jason Munn
CLIENT
Noise Pop

0646
ART DIRECTOR
Jason Munn
DESIGNER
Jason Munn
CLIENT
Chavez

0647
ART DIRECTOR
Jason Munn
DESIGNER
Jason Munn
CLIENT
Richard Goodall Gallery

0648
ART DIRECTOR
Jason Munn
DESIGNER
Jason Munn
CLIENT
The Walkmen and Noise Pop

0649
ART DIRECTOR
Jason Munn
DESIGNER
Jason Munn
CLIENT
Tortoise and Bimbo's 365 Club

0650
ART DIRECTOR
Jason Munn
DESIGNER
Jason Munn
CLIENT
The Wrens and Absolutely Kosher Records

0651
ART DIRECTOR
Jason Munn
DESIGNER
Jason Munn
CLIENT
Mates of State

0652
ART DIRECTOR
Jason Munn
DESIGNER
Jason Munn
CLIENT
Nouvelle Vague

0653
ART DIRECTOR
Jason Munn
DESIGNER
Jason Munn
CLIENT
Great American Music Hall

0654
ART DIRECTOR
Jason Munn
DESIGNER
Jason Munn
CLIENT
Matt Pond PA

0655
ART DIRECTOR
Jason Munn
DESIGNER
Jason Munn
CLIENT
Rilo Kiley and Bimbo's 365 Club

0656
ART DIRECTOR
Jason Munn
DESIGNER
Jason Munn
CLIENT
Great American Music Hall

0770
ART DIRECTOR
Jason Munn
DESIGNER
Jason Munn
CLIENT
San Francisco Museum of Modern Art and Noise Pop

0771
ART DIRECTOR
Jason Munn
DESIGNER
Jason Munn
CLIENT
Richard Goodall Gallery

0772
ART DIRECTOR
Jason Munn
DESIGNER
Jason Munn
CLIENT
The Books

Thielen Designs, Inc.

Tony Thielen
115 Gold Ave. S, Suite 209
Albuquerque, NM 87102
USA
505-205-3157

0825, 0842
ART DIRECTOR
Tony Thielen
DESIGNER
Tony Thielen
CLIENT
Hyperactive

This Way Design

Havard Gjelseth
Stensgata 40b
N-0451 Oslo
Norway
+47 41 45 46 42
hgjilseth@thiswaydesign.com

0312–0314
ART DIRECTOR
Havard Gjelseth
DESIGNER
Havard Gjelseth
CLIENT
1349

0315
ART DIRECTOR
Havard Gjelseth
DESIGNER
Havard Gjelseth
CLIENT
Seid

0829
ART DIRECTOR
Havard Gjelseth
DESIGNER
Havard Gjelseth
CLIENT
Jazzkammer

0907–0909
ART DIRECTOR
Havard Gjelseth
DESIGNER
Havard Gjelseth
CLIENT
SoNu

0910–0912
ART DIRECTORS
Havard Gjelseth, Halvor Bodin
DESIGNER
Havard Gjelseth
CLIENT
Thorns LTD

0940, 0941
ART DIRECTORS
Havard Gjelseth, Halvor Bodin
DESIGNER
Havard Gjelseth
CLIENT
King Tiki Records

Thomas Csano

3655 St-Laurent Blvd., Suite 202
Montreal, Quebec H2X 2U6
Canada
514-699-4202
Thomas@thomascsano.com

0814, 0837
ART DIRECTORS
Thomas Csano, Carlito Dalceggio, Ramachandra Borcar
DESIGNER
Thomas Csano
CLIENT
Semprini Records

Tim Gough

717 S. 19th St., #2
Philadelphia, PA 19146
USA
215-429-1154
info@timgough.org

0731, 0760
CLIENT
RS Productions

0761
ART DIRECTOR
Tim Gough
DESIGNER
Tim Gough
CLIENT
Warner Music Group

Timothy O'Donnell

322 N. Fullerton Ave.
Montclair, NJ 07042
USA
347-673-4422
timothyodo@gmail.com

0306, 0499–0502

T. Lush

Terrance Lush
P.O. Box 185143
Hamden, CT 06518
USA
203-376-6017
helloinfo@tlush.net

0274
ART DIRECTOR
Terrance Lush
DESIGNER
Terrance Lush
CLIENT
Huge Records

Tomato Kosir S.P.

Tomato Kosir
Britof 141
Kranj 4000
Slovenia
+386 41 260 979
tomato@siol.net

0740
ART DIRECTOR
Tomato Kosir
DESIGNER
Tomato Kosir

Tom Hingston Studio

Hannah Woodcock
76 Brewer St.
London W1F 9TX
UK
020 7287 6044

0045–0048
ART DIRECTOR
Tom Hingston
DESIGNER
Hannah Woodcock
CLIENT
Warner Music

0079, 0080
ART DIRECTOR
Tom Hingston
DESIGNER
Manuela Wyse
CLIENT
Kitchenware

0115–0119
ART DIRECTOR
Tom Hingston
DESIGNER
Manuela Wyse
CLIENT
Wall of Sound

0503–0505
ART DIRECTOR
Tom Hingston
DESIGNER
Danny Doyle
CLIENT
Virgin

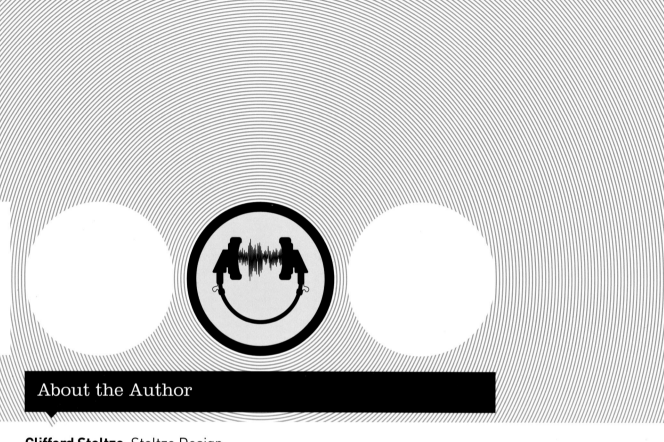

About the Author

Clifford Stoltze, Stoltze Design

Stoltze Design is a ten-person studio in Boston, Massachusetts, founded by Clifford Stoltze. Capabilities include strategic design for print, interactive media, and packaging. Over the past twenty years, Stoltze has worked with a diverse group of clients in the fields of education, publishing, technology, finance, and entertainment. His music industry clients include Sony, Capitol, EMI, Matador, and Castle von Buhler, an independent Boston label in which Stoltze was a partner.

Recognized for innovative design solutions and expressive typography, Stoltze Design has been featured in *Communication Arts, ID, How, Print, STEP inside design, Graphis,* and *Émigré Magazine* and received numerous awards from national design organizations, such as AIGA, The American Center for Design, and The Type Directors Club. Published and exhibited internationally, Stoltze's work is also in the permanent collection of the Cooper-Hewitt, National Design Museum.